WHAT WOMEN EVERYWHERE ARE SAYING ABOUT
KATHY SMITH'S LIFT WEIGHTS TO LOSE WEIGHT

"I see the changes in my body. My arms have shape, my legs are much stronger, and my abs are flat! . . . Now I like to wear sleeveless shirts and short skirts to show off my legs. Before lifting weights I was a size 10; now I'm a size 7."
—Glorymar, age 24, San Juan, Puerto Rico

"Now that I'm 43 years old, I realize that it is so important to keep my bones strong, and weight lifting is important to me for that reason. My muscle mass is probably close to what it was in my twenties. I'm sure that's one reason people think I'm younger than I really am. . . . My metabolism is running higher as well. Any extra weight I gain slips off in no time."
—Karen, Charlotte, NC

"My impression was that people who lift weights get big and bulky, and that was the last thing I wanted. . . . So far, I have lost 13 pounds and one dress size. I feel like I have more energy, and my self-confidence has gotten a tremendous boost."
—Susie, age 25, Bumpass, VA

"At 74, my waist, which was disappearing, has made a remarkable recovery and my posture has improved. Just as important, my energy level and attitude have improved. What's more, I feel good about myself, even when I look in a mirror. You can't beat that, can you?"
—Marion, Houston, TX

"I was frustrated because of my inability to lose weight through traditional aerobics. Then I discovered weight training! I went from a size 9, after having my daughter, to a size 2! I am more toned and healthier than I was before my pregnancy!"
—Brenda, age 25, Humbolt, IA

"I noticed the cellulite on the back of my legs was diminishing—something I had not been able to accomplish when doing only aerobics. Finally, at age 32, I have reached a healthy weight and am comfortable with my size."
—Tracy, Greensburg, PA

"At first I wasn't sure about weights—I thought it might be hard. Within 3 months I could see a difference. Not only did the pounds melt off, but it also defined the shape of my whole body. My energy level went sky high. Friends I hadn't seen in over six months couldn't believe how great I looked."
—T.J., age 31, Garden City, MI

"I don't have jiggling thighs anymore! I started with 5-pound dumbbells and now I'm using 12-pounders. I always feel good about myself when I am done, too!"
—Mayra, age 39, Orlando, FL

"I began to explore weight training after I became a single mom. I've been [training] 2–3 times a week and have gained increased strength and muscle definition without any bulk. At age 40, I find that I have the energy and fitness level of a woman much younger than I am."
—Deb, Chicago, IL

ALSO FROM KATHY SMITH AND WARNER BOOKS

Kathy Smith's WalkFit for a Better Body

Kathy Smith's Fitness Makeover

Kathy Smith's Getting Better All the Time

KATHY SMITH'S LIFT WEIGHTS TO LOSE WEIGHT

Kathy Smith
with Robert Miller

WARNER BOOKS

A Time Warner Company

This book is dedicated to the viewers of my *Lift Weights to Lose Weight* video who have embraced the challenge of lifting weights and are discovering for themselves the exciting benefits—both to their appearance and general health—of a simple program of strength training. In particular, I thank those who wrote to me and who have allowed me to share their personal stories in this book.

PUBLISHER'S NOTE: Neither this exercise program nor any other exercise program should be followed without first consulting a health care professional. If you have any special conditions requiring attention, you should consult with your health care professional regularly regarding possible modification of the program contained in this book.

Warner Books, Inc., 1271 Avenue of the Americas, New York, NY 10020

Visit our Web site at www.twbookmark.com

 A Time Warner Company

Printed in the United States of America

First Printing: January 2001

10 9 8

Library of Congress Cataloging-in-Publication Data

Smith, Kathy.
    [Lift weights to lose weight]
    Kathy Smith's lift weights to lose weight / by Kathy Smith.
        p. cm.
        ISBN: 978-0-446-67631-1
    1. Weight training for women. 2. Reducing exercises. 3. Physical fitness for women. I. Title.

    GV546.6. W64 S55 2001
    613.7'13—dc21   00-039901

Book design by H. Roberts Design
Cover and interior photos by Cory Sorenson
Wardrobe by Elisabetta Rogiani

Acknowledgments

The more projects I do, the more I realize that my work is a collaborative effort, and that I have been fortunate through the years to work with a great team of people. This book is no exception. I'd like to take a moment to thank some of the people who helped make this book a reality.

Rob Miller brought an extensive background in strength and weight training projects—not to mention his great writing skills. A gentle soul with the gift of being a terrific listener, he demonstrated an incredible ability to organize and craft all the disjointed pieces of information generated in our conversations while keeping his sense of humor—and mine.

Douglas Brooks and Candace Copeland once again came through with flying colors. They've contributed their technical expertise to past projects, and their insight and creative ideas never cease to amaze me. Their commitment to promoting a healthy lifestyle and living what they preach always commands my respect.

Russ Kamalski once again earned his stripes as the coordinator of this book. He's been by my side now for nearly ten years, and I have enjoyed every minute. A sound businessman with an incredibly artistic and creative side, he has my enduring respect and thanks.

Diana Baroni at Warner Books joined me for the second time as my editor. She helped focus my thoughts on this project and supported the key decisions we made along the way. Her editing advice, as always, was right on the mark.

Cory Sorenson helped take all the text and make it visual. His discerning eye behind the camera brought a creative vision to the photography. A special thanks goes to Bodies In Motion, for providing the stage for our photo shoot.

Jerry Robinson, whose *Secrets of Advanced Bodybuilders* was a valuable resource in writing this book, has through the years taught me not only the broader concepts of weight training, but also the more subtle nuances.

Bonnie Modugno, M.S., R.D., provided the basis for the nutritional information presented here, as well as the 1-2-3 Plan.

And to all my workout partners through the years—whether professional colleagues like Rick Bernstein or personal friends like Fran and Laurine—for helping to keep me inspired in my workouts—thank you.

Finally, thanks to Steve, Kate, and Perrie, for putting up with my crazy work schedule and bringing such joy to my life.

Contents

Introduction: Weight Lifting Is for Everyone! *ix*

Chapter 1   The Big Shift to Strength Training   *1*

Chapter 2   Lift Weights to Lose Weight . . . and *Much More!*   *9*

Chapter 3   The Ideal Body: Yours!   *17*

Chapter 4   A Look Inside   *25*

Chapter 5   Exercise Basics   *39*

Chapter 6   Your Routine   *49*

Chapter 7   Home Is Where the Gym Is   *59*

Chapter 8   Making It Happen   *73*

Chapter 9   Warm Up and Stretch   *85*

Chapter 10   Your Strength Training Program   *99*

    The Exercises   *101*

    12-Week Program and Training Log   *224*

Chapter 11   Fuel Up and Slim Down   *251*

    Nutritional Journal   *264*

Chapter 12   A Lifetime Prescription   *273*

Appendix A   *Kathy Smith's Lift Weights to Lose Weight*
    12-Week Promise   *281*

Appendix B   Meal Planner   *285*

Index   *287*

About the Author   *292*

Weight Lifting Is for Everyone!

What *is* it about women and weights?

To this day, I see magazine articles recommending that women train their muscles by lifting 1-pound soup cans or bottles of water. Excuse me—soup cans? I find this silly, even a bit insulting. A 1-pound weight might be the place to *start,* if you're extremely weak. But if you want to build strength to help you in daily life, it's not enough. How much sense does it make to train with 1-pound soup cans, when the grocery bag you're bringing them home in probably weighs at least 8 pounds?

Let's face it: No one would ever tell a *man* to lift canned food! Certainly no serious athlete would train that way. Women, though, have always been timid about weights, and these watered-down substitutes are the result. Even though an average day makes hundreds of demands on our strength, there's an unspoken assumption (which many women unconsciously buy into) that women won't take the trouble to understand the benefits of weight training and learn how to do it properly.

It's Time for a Change!

Frankly, if we took the same timid approach in other areas of life that we take with strength training, we'd still be back in the 1950s, doing housework in high heels. Women today are running corporations, going into space, supporting families, sitting on the Supreme Court—we've proven our capabilities again and again. For us to shrink from the idea of lifting weights is simply old-fashioned.

Even the very word "strength" is still waiting for women to claim it. Until now, we've embraced terms like "toned" or "defined." Why not *strong?* It's time for women to discover that we can be strong without sacrificing feminine traits. Softness and strength can co-exist—and it's when they *do* that you have the fullest, richest experience of life.

Here's the Plan...

In this book, you'll learn about the many good reasons why strength training is not merely beneficial, but imperative! You'll learn why it's an essential part of a balanced fitness program, and why it becomes more important the older you get.

With the help of the simple program in this book, you'll get to experience all that strength training has to offer. Together, you and I will work through the following stages:

• **Envision the possibilities.**
We'll talk about how weight training can fit into your life and what it can do for you.

• **Learn the ropes.**
I'll take you through the basics of muscle anatomy, fat reduction, and the principles of lifting weights and putting together a routine. And I'll explain exactly how to use the routines and log pages in this book.

• **Make a painless 12-week "mini-commitment."**
Once we've covered the principles involved, I'll invite you to conduct a fun, 12-week experiment with weight training. I'll urge you to make a pledge to yourself to complete this 12-week introduction, so that you'll have the chance to judge the results in your own body.

• **Find and equip your space.**
The decision of whether to train at home or in a health club can have a big influence on your success. I'll help you choose the setting that fits your personality, and introduce you to the basic equipment involved.

• **Figure out how to make it work.**

We've all experienced it—that all-too-human tendency to drop the ball somewhere around Week 3. That's why, in the chapter called "Making It Happen," I'll give you strategies to ensure your success, including tricks for organizing your time and motivating yourself so that your good intentions have a chance to bear fruit.

• **Supplement your efforts with proper nutrition—as easy as 1, 2, 3!**

Effective weight management is far more effective when you supplement your exercise regimen with good eating habits. My 1-2-3 Plan is not a diet, but a simple framework you can follow to put together healthy meals that won't leave you feeling deprived!

• **Aim for integration.**

Sweeping change is the sum of small choices we make every day. We'll talk about how to gradually adopt a healthier lifestyle that you can live with over the long run.

Throughout this book, you'll find testimonials from women who've used the routines on my *Lift Weights to Lose Weight* video and who describe how their perspective has changed as they've had a personal experience with weight lifting.

Success Is Habit Forming

This book is designed to give you the knowledge and tools necessary to create positive change. But that's just the beginning. Yes, learning the principles of weight training will enable you to train more easily and efficiently. But it's a woman's consummate desire, her passion for the outcome, that gives her the energy to reach her goal.

That's why it's my purpose not just to educate you, but to motivate you as well—and, more importantly, guide you into a personal experience that will motivate you from *within*. I'll help you visualize the wide range of benefits of lifting weights, and I'll show you how easy it is to attain them. Hopefully, you'll take that one important step of faith—the 12-week commitment that is the heart of this program.

Once you're on your way, strength training becomes a self-motivating process. Being stronger feels good, and your success will be habit-forming. The more you get, the more you'll want. So let's get started!

The Big Shift to Strength Training

20 Years of Aerobics, and We Still Don't Have the Bodies We Want!

Let me tell you a story about Madeline.

Madeline Lewis, my choreographer, whom I've worked with on videos for 20 years, is a great example of a phenomenon I know many women are experiencing.

Madeline is 40 and, far from being merely a casual exerciser, she has *taught* aerobics for most of her life. She could probably dance rings around most of us, thanks to her very high level of aerobic fitness. Yet, in recent years (and especially since her pregnancy), she's noticed a significant loss of upper body muscle tone. Even more perplexing, given all the cardio she does, she's gaining weight!

Maybe you've had the same experience: years of sweating through cardio classes, really putting in the time, but not getting the results you used to. Women are constantly coming to me and saying, "Kathy, I've been walking on my treadmill every day for two years, and I just can't lose any weight."

Clearly, something's not right. Routines that once kept us slim and fit don't seem to be working anymore. Even for many women in their twenties, aerobics alone just isn't doing the trick. It doesn't make sense: All that cardio *must* still be burning calories. What's going on?

Muscle Mass

First of all, I realize *muscle mass* may not be a term you like to apply to your own body. It sounds a bit too much like "massive muscles." But muscle mass simply refers to the total amount of muscle in your body. And it's a *good* thing. A very good thing.

Lean body mass, or muscle mass, gives your body firmness and shape. It allows you to move with strength and power. And it's the engine that burns calories and keeps you looking slim.

As we move from our twenties into our early thirties, an important (and unfortunate!) change occurs in our bodies: We begin to lose skeletal muscle mass. Although genetic factors play a role in this, the main culprit is the sedentary lifestyle we tend to adopt as we get older and the fact that our normal daily activities just don't adequately challenge our muscles. Whatever muscle we had in our twenties thus begins a slow process of wasting away that continues for the rest of our life. Studies show a woman may lose up to *one third of her muscle* between ages 35 and 80!

Loss of muscle sets off a chain reaction:

• We become weaker.
From age 40 on, a woman may lose 10 to 20 percent of her strength with each passing decade.

• We become less active.
Having less muscle makes it harder to stay active; less activity accelerates the wasting of muscles, and the downward spiral goes on.

• We lose bone density.
Your bones need the load-bearing demands of regular exercise to stay healthy. Inactivity allows bones to become thinner and more fragile.

• We experience a drop in metabolic rate.
Muscle tissue burns calories day and night, awake or asleep. If you lose muscle, you reduce the capacity of your body's calorie-burning engine, and excess calories get stored as fat. Dieting makes it worse by depressing your metabolism further.

• We exchange muscle for fat.
Even if your weight doesn't change, your body may undergo a steady shift in body composition, as your muscles waste away and new fat is stored.

The good news is, this scenario only describes what *would* happen if you did nothing to preserve your body's lean muscle mass.

Reversing the Trend: The Sooner the Better

> *"I was frustrated because of my inability to lose weight through traditional aerobics. Then I discovered weight training! I went from a size 9, after having my daughter, to a size 2! I am more toned and healthier than I was before my pregnancy!"*
> **Brenda, age 25**
> **Humboldt, IA**

Clearly, it's vital to do everything possible to hold on to lean muscle mass. Preserve your muscle and you can prevent this chain of events—especially the metabolic slump that leads to weight gain. And the time to start is now. Even if you're still in your twenties, working to increase your muscle mass *now* will bring both immediate and long-term benefits. Not only will it help deter the problems I've described from occurring in the future, it will also help you improve the shape of your body and reduce fat right now. Women of all ages should make muscle mass a priority! The question is: *How?*

Aerobics Alone Won't Do It

Doing aerobic exercise burns calories and may elevate your metabolism for a short time afterward. But the thing that really keeps your metabolism cooking is muscle. The more muscle, the greater your caloric-burning potential. Unfortunately, while aerobic work improves the *tone* of the muscles you're using (usually your leg muscles), it won't induce them to maintain their size.

Second, since aerobic exercise focuses on large muscle groups of the lower body, it allows upper body areas like the chest, upper arms, and shoulders to lose both fullness *and* tone over time.

At best, as a cardio veteran in your forties, you've retained lower body tone. You may have kept your weight under control, but your body is storing more fat as the age-related loss of muscle slows your metabolism and makes it harder to burn calories. Life events such as pregnancy, menopause, or other interruptions in your training only speed the process.

You end up, like Madeline, with great cardiovascular endurance, some tone in your legs, but smaller muscles overall, poor upper body tone, and more fat.

The Solution Is *Muscle*

Numerous recent studies have demonstrated the value of strength training for building muscle and reducing fat. In one study, women lost an average of 8 pounds of fat in two months just by lifting light weights three times a week to increase muscle mass.

This suggests that a significant portion of your workout time should be dedicated to strength training. I've made over two dozen aerobics videos in my life and spent countless hours doing aerobics. I would never want to have to choose, but if I could only do one form of training from now on, I'd give up cardio and focus on weight training.

That's a strong statement! Of course, I'm not suggesting anyone give up aerobics. Still, from about age 30 on, strength training becomes more important with each passing year. Your goal should be to find a balance of strength and cardio that makes sense for your age and fitness goals. Everyone, by age 40, should be devoting at least 20 to 30 minutes 2 to 3 times a week to strength training. Of course, the sooner you start, the better, because the more muscle you have going into your thirties and forties, the easier it will be to retain it.

CAN'T TRUST THE SCALE

As the years go by, you can actually find yourself putting on fat, and perhaps a dress size or two, even though your weight is about the same as ever. Compact muscle tissue has been replaced by lighter, bulkier fat tissue—a poor trade that the scale won't reveal.

For example, a lean, 25-year-old woman might weigh 125 pounds, with 18 percent body fat. By age 40, the same woman might still weigh roughly 125 pounds, but now with 25 to 26 percent body fat. Because fat tissue is bulkier than lean muscle, her dress size has stretched from a 6 to a 10 during these years of muscle loss. The good news is, this process can be turned around, but aerobic training alone won't do it.

The Benefits of Strength Training

Chapter 2 will go into much more detail about what you can expect to gain from regular strength training, but here's a sampling of the benefits:

For your appearance:
- a shapelier physique
- improved muscle tone and firmness
- increased lean mass; higher metabolism helping you to burn more calories
- improved posture and movement

For your general health:
- stronger bones to prevent osteoporosis and bone fractures
- stronger heart
- lower blood pressure

For your mind:
- increased self-reliance
- a mental break
- reduced stress

As you can see, losing weight is just one of many reasons to lift weights!

And what about my friend Madeline? She finally began a weight lifting program. Although it's been only a few months, she's seeing such great results she wonders why she waited so long!

Taming the Cardio Animal and Teaching Her New Tricks

The cardio scene has been going strong for about 20 years. In that time, most of us have managed to work some form of aerobic training into our lives. Whether it's high-impact aerobics, stepping, or spinning, we've come to thrive on the group energy, the shared goal to sweat and burn calories, the endorphin high—all these things keep us coming back for more. In other words, we've succeeded in making cardio fun.

So far, though, there's very little organized *fun* around lifting weights. True, we've introduced weights into classes using light dumbbells for, say, 5 minutes at the end of a cardio session. And, in some parts of the country, studios have experimented with "pump classes" that promote lifting in a group setting. Trouble is, these classes often don't include much basic instruction, so they don't give beginners an easy way in.

Your best course is to approach weight training on an individual basis. I created this program to help you do that—and do it in a way I think you'll find easy *and* fun! There are two basic principles behind this book, which I'll devote the rest of the chapter to discussing.

"I have always battled with my weight and a feeling of being fat. I [exercised] and watched my diet, but my weight still fluctuated. About three years ago, I added weights to my routine. I have gone from a size 8 to a size 4—even though my weight is about 130–135. Since I began weight training I sleep better at night, my stress level is reduced, I have more energy, I feel stronger, and my body burns food more efficiently. I feel great, and when talking to friends about my success I always mention the benefits of using weights."
Tonya-Sue
Warren, CT

STEP 1: BELIEF IN THE GOAL
Femininity and Muscle

I have women say to me: "I don't want to look like those body-builders," and I laugh and say, "Just try! Do you know how hard they work, and what they put their bodies through?" I think it's hysterical that women are afraid of looking like that from one or two workouts a week! —PAIGE, PERSONAL TRAINER

Many women—even the fervent "cardio animals"—still view weights with a skeptical eye. Most objections are based on traditional stereotypes and misunderstanding. The first step, then, is to open your mind to possibilities. Weight lifting is for everyone!

Perhaps at one time or another you've seen competitive female bodybuilders with bulging, cut physiques, protruding veins and single-digit body

MYTHS AND MISCONCEPTIONS: WHAT'S YOUR EXCUSE?

I don't want to build up my muscles, because if I stop training, the muscle will all turn to fat.

Muscle doesn't *literally* turn to fat; they're completely different kinds of tissue. If you stop training, the muscle will gradually waste away, and fat may start to accumulate simply because your body is using fewer calories. The solution: Don't stop training!

I know I'm overweight, but I gain muscle easily, and exercise will just make me bulkier.

Your body has only one way to get rid of fat, and that's to burn it. The more muscle you have, the easier it is for your body to burn fat. Although a little extra muscle might make you feel larger at first, it's the fastest way to get your weight down and ensure a shapely, toned physique.

Lifting weights will make me appear masculine.

Muscle mass naturally peaks for women in their twenties. Would you say 20-year-old women look more "masculine" than women in their forties who've lost much of that muscle? Think of weight training as simply a way to recapture the shapely firmness that age-related muscle loss takes away. Your genetic makeup and a moderate approach to training will ensure that you won't gain excessive bulk.

fat—and thought, "There! *That's* what lifting weights does to a woman."

Well, hardly! There is a small minority of women whose genetics are especially suited to gaining muscle. Still, any competitive bodybuilder will tell you that to achieve these results requires a grueling training regimen. And what she probably *won't* tell you is that such extreme development is also usually the result of dangerous performance-enhancing drugs, including anabolic steroids and other hormones, aimed at mimicking the *male* tendency to build muscle.

The Role of Hormones

Generally speaking, women don't have the physiological makeup to experience large increases in muscle size. That's because muscle building depends on various growth-producing hormones, specifically *testosterone*.

High levels of testosterone create the secondary characteristics we think of as masculine: deep voice, body hair, stronger odors. Although women's testosterone levels vary (as do men's), men still have 20 to 30 times more testosterone than women. Moderate weight lifting sessions simply will not turn you into anything even *resembling* a bodybuilder.

What You Can Expect

Nature is geared to maintain the line between the sexes, and ensure that women continue to look like women. Men and women will each experience changes through strength training, but a woman's changes will occur in relation to female physiology.

Women who lift weights can expect to develop shapely, trim, *feminine* figures. The lower your body fat, the greater your muscular definition. But a woman's big fear, of developing excessive bulk—it's just not going to happen!

That's not to say that it's impossible to become more muscular than you would *want* to be. I think a lot of trainers and authors go too far in suggesting that women simply won't gain muscle, period. They should read my mail! I get countless letters from women, saying things like: "Kathy, I've been doing just two sessions of squats a week and my legs are getting so big—help!"

I experience this myself. For me, it's my back muscles. I'll do Lat Pull-downs for a little while and suddenly my bras, shirts, sweaters, *everything* is too tight—the buttons pop open and I can't wear them. So don't tell me you can't build muscle—you can! The important thing is to keep these changes in perspective.

Training Strategies to Suit Individual Needs

Some women (just like some men) gain muscle more easily, depending on the amount of testosterone their body naturally produces. Athletic body types will generally have an easier time gaining muscle. But growth will still occur within the limits of female physiology. Even an athletic body type will require significant time and effort to build an athletic physique.

A moderate weight lifting program like the one in this book will, for most women, produce only slight changes in muscle size—just enough to give your body the shape you want and help you realize the many health benefits of a leaner body composition.

If you are among the small minority who find they need to train more conservatively to avoid gaining bulk, Chapter 5 contains information on how to adjust your rep numbers and resistance to do this and still get the toning benefits you want.

> "My impression was that people who lift weights get big and bulky, and that was the last thing I wanted. In doing a little research, I discovered how lifting weights could boost your energy and metabolism. So far, I have lost 13 pounds and one dress size. I feel like I have more energy, and my self-confidence has gotten a tremendous boost."
> **Susie, age 25**
> **Bumpass, VA**

STEP 2: OVERCOMING THE INTIMIDATION FACTOR

While easy to learn, weight lifting does require some knowledge of basic principles, including how your muscles work, proper lifting technique, and how to put together a routine and schedule your workouts. All this can make it seem a little scary at first—especially since, without the support of a class setting, the burden of overcoming the intimidation factor rests on you.

Once upon a time—in the early 1970s—Nautilus clubs offered an easy way to get some of the benefits of weight lifting. All you had to do was work your way along a predetermined line of machines and, in 20 minutes, you were out the door. While limited in some ways, it was a simple and inviting way to package strength training. Nowadays, though, things are

MUSCLE AND FEMININITY: KEEPING IT IN PERSPECTIVE

From talking with my husband and other male friends, I find there's a difference in the way men and women assess changes in their muscularity. Men measure their muscle development in *inches*, and unless their new muscle is visible at twenty paces, they're not satisfied. Not so with women. We're much more sensitive to tiny increases. Muscle growth that's scarcely visible may change the way a blouse or a bra feels. It's important to remember that, even if you start to feel your clothes fitting differently, it's probably a very slight change in objective terms. Sometimes change of any kind (even change for the better) takes a little getting used to!

I was born with an athletic body. Because of my genetics, weight training does increase the size of my muscles, and sometimes I have to throttle back a little so that my blouses don't get too tight in the shoulders. But, even at my most developed (as you'll see if you watch my *Lift Weights to Lose Weight* video) I've never felt the slightest bit less feminine!

more complicated. You may walk into a new gym and see fifty or more machines, with no instructions or diagrams to give the beginner any help—or even a clue to what part of the body each one works!

Of course, personal trainers are a great way to go, if you have the means. One way or another, though, it's vital to learn the basics to ensure that you get an effective workout in the least amount of time, with the least risk of injury.

That's where my *Lift Weights to Lose Weight* program comes in. Whether you decide to work out in a gym or in the privacy of your home, this book will be your map, your self-guided tour. I'll be with you each step of the way, and by the end you'll have the knowledge and self-confidence to be your own coach and guide.

Because weight training isn't a group activity, it requires a bit more of *you*. And that's good, because it means when you succeed, you really have yourself to thank! Plus, you'll feel a surge of self-reliance that will carry over into other areas of life. It's all part of the magic that happens when you stop making excuses, and start making changes. And, with the guidelines in this program to keep you on track, I promise it will be easy *and* fun!

In the next chapter, we'll begin to focus more clearly on our goals, and discuss in more detail the wide range of benefits you can expect from strength training.

Lift Weights to Lose Weight . . . and *Much More!*

What made you pick up this book? I'll bet it was the goal of losing weight, right there in the title. After all, lifting weights is not exactly a natural activity. Unlike walking, it's not something you'd do without a good reason.

This book is called *Lift Weights to Lose Weight*, but a slimmer figure is only one of the many things you'll *gain* by lifting weights. I realize you may be preoccupied just now with those extra pounds. But let's take a few minutes to look at the big picture. I'm sure you've had the experience of stopping during a workout, sweat trickling down your nose, and asking yourself: *"Why am I doing this?"*

Well, the more strong, compelling reasons you have for doing something, the more likely you are to do it.

13 Strong Reasons to Lift Weights

First and foremost, strength training builds muscle.

Why do I need more muscle? you ask. Remember in the last chapter I described the downhill slide that occurs when you begin to *lose* muscle tissue? With each passing year, you become weaker, less active, and you store more fat.

Strength training reverses that trend, and starts a positive chain of events. By lifting weights, you:

- gain strength
- become more active
- increase your metabolism

These three changes will trigger a wide range of positive effects. Let's go through them one by one:

> *"I have found weight training to be the fastest, most efficient way to tone and add precise definition to the body. I measure my success by looking at my muscle tone and the way my clothing fits. [Weight training] has made me feel younger, sharper, stronger, and more energized than I have in years."*
> Irene, age 44
> Ocala, FL

Higher Metabolism and Fat Loss

You hear the term "metabolism" more and more these days. Ever wonder just what it is, and why a *higher* one is better? Here's how it works:

Metabolism refers to the overall exchange of energy within your body. Food goes in, and your body transforms it into energy, fueling all your internal processes. If "energy in" equals "energy out," everything's fine. But often our metabolic needs are lower than our energy intake. We eat more calories than we use. When that happens, the excess is stored as fat.

Muscle burns the excess calories two ways: First, during the actual exertion of exercise. Second, and even more important, our muscle tissue burns calories all day long. Even at rest, muscles are gobbling calories. In fact, each new pound of lean muscle raises your metabolism by an extra 50 calories a day *just by being there*. Greater muscle mass helps you lose weight without severe dietary restrictions—or, looking at it another way, it means you can eat a greater number of calories without fear of *gaining* weight.

Stronger Bones

Your bones don't have to become frail as you age. New research shows that the stresses of exercise play a powerful role in keeping your bones dense and strong.

It's another case of "use it or lose it." Although your bones are always working to counteract the pull of gravity, it's the greater load they support during exercise that really stimulates them to grow and remain strong. The effect is very specific: Tennis players, for instance, develop greater bone density specifically in their racquet arm!

Aerobic activities, including running, walking, and even swimming, all stimulate bone growth to different degrees—but the more load or force involved, the better. That's why weight lifting, combined with weight-bearing aerobic activity, is the best way to maintain the bone density you have, and possibly even reverse some of the bone loss that occurs with age.

More Strength for Daily Tasks

Let's get practical: Being stronger is just darn useful. The extra strength and endurance you gain from weight training makes hundreds of tasks in your daily life easier. Carrying groceries upstairs, wrestling with the daybed in the guest room, twisting the lid off that pickle jar—it all requires strength.

You might wonder: With so many feats of strength built into my average day, why am I not *already* strong enough to make them seem easy?

Here's the reason: Daily tasks only seem easier once you've become *stronger than you need to be* to do them. This is what training with weights will do. Weight training is a safe, efficient way to create well-balanced overall strength that will be useful in all situations. Then, you can tackle your daily chores with strength and muscular endurance *in reserve.* Next time you're lifting the baby carrier out of the back seat for the fourth time in one morning, believe me, you'll notice the difference!

> *"Lifting weights has improved my posture. For ten years, I have had a tendency to hunch over rather than sit up or stand straight. Weight training has strengthened my back muscles so that correct posture now comes naturally."*
> **Sharla, age 39**
> **Midland, TX**

Body Shaping

The older I get, the more I appreciate weight training's ability to tighten, tone, and reshape specific areas of the body. Whether it's hamstring and glute exercises to lift the butt, or triceps exercises to firm the backs of the arms, weight lifting lets you zero right in on the problem areas. Although women aren't likely to experience large increases in muscle size, the slight increases that occur—as well as the striking improvement in tone—are enough to make a big difference in the way you look and feel.

You can also use weight training to add symmetry to your body as a whole. For instance, a woman with a "pear-shaped" physique—whose shoulders are narrower than her hips—could use weight training to enhance her upper body. Or, a woman whose legs are naturally well developed in front might use weights to contour the back of her thighs and buttocks, creating a more shapely and balanced profile.

Stronger Joints Make Aerobic Exercise Easier

Lifting weights is one of the best things you can do to help your aerobic training. Jumping right into an aerobics program, if you've never exercised before, can be a major shock to your body. Particularly if you're overweight, the repetitive impact can tax your joints and force you to stop long before you've gotten much benefit. It's a catch-22: In a sense, you're not fit enough to exercise effectively!

Weight training is the perfect solution. Because it's nonimpact exercise, it lets you strengthen muscles and connective tissues without straining them. Then, when you do begin walking, jogging, or cycling, you'll find it much easier and a lot more fun.

This benefit continues beyond the beginning level, too. Keeping your joints strong with weight training is a great way to ensure your ability to train aerobically at the highest possible level without strain.

A WORD ON GOAL SETTING: BE POSITIVE!

An important part of answering the question "Why am I doing this?" is to define your goal in positive terms. Goals become more real to us when we express them in terms of "getting" rather than "losing" or "giving up." Giving up dessert, for instance, paints a picture in your head of deprivation, of missing out on something you enjoy. On the other hand, attending your high school reunion in your favorite sleeveless dress paints a very different picture. Now you're *getting* something positive—in this case, the personal satisfaction of feeling attractive and confident.

So, instead of "losing weight," decide that what you're *really* doing is trading away excess fat for a long list of *specific benefits* that will improve, not just your appearance, but your health, longevity, and quality of life.

Protection from Injury

Life is full of little hazards—a box on the top shelf that turns out to be heavier than you thought, a wrinkle in the rug or a step you didn't see, a slippery floor, a desk chair that scoots out from under you. How well you fare depends on your body's ability to roll with the punches: to apply force here, absorb shock there. All that depends on muscle.

Strengthening muscle makes your whole body more sturdy. It does this by fortifying three kinds of tissue associated with your muscles:

- the tendons that connect them to your bones
- the ligaments that hold your joints together
- the bones themselves

Weight training can also improve balance and coordination. When hazards pop up, there's a better chance you'll be able to sidestep, dodge, or otherwise recover. If you do take a spill, chances are you'll land more like a cat, and less like a stack of dishes.

Better Posture

I'll make a prediction: At some point before the fourth or fifth week of this program, people are going to start telling you that you look...different. They may think you're looking taller, thinner, more confident; the truth is, it's your posture.

Often, even before the other effects of weight training become visible, they become apparent in the way you hold your body and carry yourself. Good posture depends on the strength, endurance, and flexibility of the muscles of the back, shoulders, and abdomen. Even a small amount of weight training is enough to cause changes in your nervous system that help these muscles do their job more effectively.

Proper carriage can make you look thinner, too. If you're concerned about that little accumulation of fat around your middle, part of the solution is just learning to stay lifted in that area. Standing up straight can go a long way toward helping create a longer, leaner appearance.

Relief from Low Back Pain

Ever been laid up with back pain? You're certainly not alone: 80 percent of Americans experience it at some time in their lives. Back pain is often triggered innocently by an afternoon of gardening, or stooping for the morning paper, but it's most likely caused by a gradual weakening of the spine and supporting muscles from years of poor support.

Making sure you have properly supportive furniture can help, but the first line of defense against spinal stress should be your body's own architecture. Specifically, it's the combination of spinal muscles and abdominal muscles that hold your spine in good alignment when standing and sitting, and which support your spine when you're bending or lifting. Weight training helps them do this. It also helps prevent back injuries by strengthening the vertebrae themselves.

> "I feel so much better since I started lifting weights. People keep telling me I look better, I have more energy—less of the 'blahs.' I don't want to go back to feeling sluggish and mopey. And I love having muscles that I can see!"
> Kathy, age 46
> Naperville, IL

Improved Skin Quality

I get a lot of compliments on my skin tone. One secret is to not put your skin through the wear and tear of wide fluctuations in weight. Because skin loses elasticity as we age, cycles of weight gain and dieting stretch the skin and then leave it hanging. Instead of dieting down to "skin and bones," a much better solution is to replace at least some portion of whatever fat you may have with a moderate amount of shapely, lean muscle. A program of cardio and strength training combined with sensible eating will help you do that and preserve a tight, youthful skin tone.

A Healthier Heart

Everyone knows aerobic exercise is good for your heart—that's why we call it "cardio." But aerobic training isn't the only way to help your heart. Researchers are finding that strength training can play a role, too. Weight lifting improves your muscle-to-fat ratio, making your body leaner, and putting less stress on the heart muscle. A leaner body also has beneficial effects on blood pressure, and can improve blood lipid profiles by raising your level of HDLs (the good cholesterol).

A Mental Lift

I can personally speak for the power of exercise to heal depression: I began running during college as a way of coping with the sudden loss of my parents. The benefits were so great that exercise has become my lifelong passion. The mood-lifting properties of aerobics have, I'm sure, been felt by anyone who has exercised consistently for a few weeks or more.

Weight training, too, seems to have a strong antidepressant effect, probably by building feelings of self-efficacy and providing a sense of accomplishment. Scientific studies bear this out. In one, researchers at Tufts University and Penn State University put a group of women in their eighties and nineties through a 10-week exercise program. As you might imagine, people in this age group often suffer depression due to incapacity. Not only did their weight lifting ability improve by 118 percent, but these new strength trainers became less depressed, more social, and showed more interest in group activities. (*New England Journal of Medicine*, June 23, 1994.)

It makes sense: People become depressed when their capabilities are diminished—by age, illness, or other factors. It stands to reason that finding yourself stronger and able to do more will reduce depression and increase your enjoyment of life.

Stress Reduction

This happens to me all the time: I'll start the day with a tight schedule. Then, something unpredictable happens—having two kids guarantees that!—and I get behind. From then on, I'm feeling stressed and under pressure.

That's a day when you'd probably skip your workout, right? Not me! I head straight for the gym. My training partner and I laugh and have a good time; it becomes a wonderful psychological escape. Instead of obsessing about my problems, my kids, or my schedule, I'm just focusing on that hamstring, visualizing the muscle contracting as I curl my leg. Half an hour later I'm back in the fray of everyday life and I feel great.

My philosophy is that *life pressures will always be there.* I don't think of my workout as just another duty that eats up time. I think of it as the antidote for the stress I'm under. If you're feeling a lack of control in your life, it puts you right back in charge.

Self-Reliance and Personal Power

Discovering that you *can* meet the challenge of a weight workout will give you a feeling of self-reliance that can carry into other areas of life. A friend told me, "Once I'd had the experience of lifting a weight, it became a symbol of my personal power that I can access anytime I feel a little over-whelmed or intimidated—if I have to confront my boss, for instance. Instead of worrying about it and focusing on my butterflies, I visualize myself 'confronting' a barbell, or a weight stack." Standing outside her boss's office, my friend would picture herself preparing for a lift: focusing all her attention on the weight, taking a deep breath, centering her body, and feeling the strength gathering in her limbs. *Then* she'd knock on the door.

That may sound far-fetched until you've experienced it yourself. Physical, sensory experiences are very powerful. Once you've felt what it's like to confront a physical challenge—such as a heavy weight—focus your attention and your strength on it in a direct, efficient way, *and make it move*…it's tremendously empowering! And you really can draw on that power anytime you choose to.

Even though weight loss may be the emotional button you're responding to at the moment, weight training offers a panorama of benefits, especially when combined with aerobic conditioning, flexibility, and sensible eating. Imagine being not just slimmer, but stronger, healthier, more confident, youthful, and fully alive—year in and year out!

In the next chapter, we'll take a look at your body's unique characteristics and discuss what type of program will be best for you.

Chapter 3

The Ideal Body: Yours!

I've been on the board of the Women's Sports Foundation for five years now. It's a great group, started by Billie Jean King. By providing grants and lobbying in Congress, the foundation devotes itself to promoting sports and fitness among young women.

Every year at our big dinner we have an event called the Parade of Champions, in which 100 female athletes take the stage to be honored. These women represent just about every sport under the sun—soccer, basketball, water skiing, billiards, judo—you name it.

What a variety of physiques! Tall, lean figure skaters, muscular gymnasts, lanky basketball players—no two are alike. But here's what I find so interesting, and so inspiring: Tall, short, thick, or thin, all of them walk onto that stage with a palpable confidence and poise. They may *look* different, but they're all champions, because each has made the most of the gifts she has.

There's No One Ideal

This is really a great time to be a woman. More than ever before in history, society is opening up to the idea of well-developed female bodies—

INFINITE VARIETY . . .

Here are just some of the ways humans differ from one another, right from the starting line:

Hormones: The amount of certain hormones your body produces, such as testosterone or growth hormone, can have a huge impact on how your body responds to training.

Type and Distribution of Muscle: Some muscle fibers in your body are engineered for strength, others for endurance. Whatever ratio you have of these two types will affect your performance, making some activities easier than others.

Body Fat: The amount and distribution of body fat affects your appearance, athletic ability, and health.

Postural Abnormalities: Genetic curvatures of the spine such as scoliosis (a sideways curvature) or hyperlordosis (swayback) probably mean you'll have to pay special attention to your form when exercising. Some postural problems can be addressed through strength training.

Center of Gravity: The distribution of weight on your body can affect your ability to balance.

Body Type: Differences in the basic shape of your body are associated with a wide range of physical strengths and limitations.

Existing Injuries or Other Physical Conditions: Knee surgeries, back problems, or other physical conditions or health problems may affect your energy level or your ability to perform certain motions.

Prior Experience: If you've already mastered the basic mechanics of training, you may progress faster than someone who's starting from scratch. On the other hand, poor form can limit your results and may cause injury, so it's a good idea to double-check to be sure you've got it right.

Of course, not all differences mean that you have to train differently. After all, some of these factors are things you might not even be aware of. Still, your unique characteristics may affect the results your training will produce, and should, where possible, be taken into account in setting your expectations.

of strong, fit women. Little by little, we're redefining "femininity" to include athletic power and skill.

Part of this coming of age, though, is the need to accept that we're all different. Despite whatever physique Hollywood may be selling at the moment, the fact is, there's no one ideal body; no standard we should all try to fit.

Do this: Close your eyes and think about your own body. Visualize your height, the width of your shoulders, the width of your hips, the length of your arms, legs, and neck. Spend a long moment trying to see yourself as you really are. Now imagine what you might do to improve the shape, the tone, and the health of *your particular, God-given body.*

For instance, you may be 5 foot 3, but perhaps a slimmer waist and improved posture would help give your body a sense of greater proportionality and stature. No matter what sort of basic physical characteristics you've been blessed with, being stronger and more fit will help you feel more confident, and more fulfilled. So don't just cut out a picture of some model or movie star you want to look like. *Create* the picture—of yourself.

In this chapter we'll talk about individual differences, and how to develop goals and expectations that fit your unique physical gifts.

The plan, quite simply, should be to become the best possible *you.*

Body Types:
Which Type Are You?

Remember I said we come in all shapes and sizes? The system of body types (also called *somatotypes*) commonly used in scientific and medical circles was developed in the 1950s by W. H. Sheldon and provides a convenient way of classifying the structural and performance differences between people. According to this system, there are three basic types: the slender *ectomorph,* the athletic *mesomorph,* and the soft *endomorph.* Each has its strengths and limits.

Most people don't fit perfectly into any one type. However, as you read through the descriptions, I'll bet you'll be able to relate characteristics of one or more types to yourself or someone you know.

> "At 5 foot 1 I can't afford to gain weight—just 5 pounds can send me to the clothing store for a new wardrobe. Aerobics is wonderful for your heart, but you won't keep weight off with that alone. Lifting weights gives me a firm body but most importantly it gives me a sense that I'm strong. It makes me feel like I am in control of my body."
> **Kim, age 36**
> **Edenton, NC**

The Ectomorph:
Thin, Little Fat or Muscle

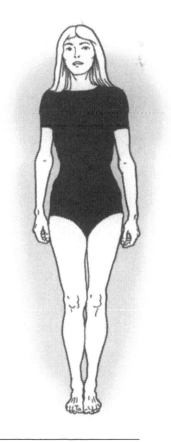

Ectomorphs have long, narrow, lean, lithe, angular bodies. Their muscles and connective tissues are loose, allowing more flexibility and mobility than other body types, and this general looseness and lack of muscle makes them more likely to have poor posture. Proportionately, ectomorphs are fine-boned, with narrow shoulders, a flat chest, and long limbs. What little fat they carry accumulates in the hips and thighs.

Ectomorphs tend to have inefficient cardiovascular systems and may have problems with low blood pressure, high heart rate, poor circulation, dizziness on standing, and poor endurance. They gain muscle slowly and with difficulty.

A well-developed and efficient nervous system makes ectomorphs highly sensitive and adept at activities requiring speed of movement. On the other hand, they have inefficient digestive systems, which helps them to stay thin but may leave them prone to hypoglycemia. There's also some evidence that ectomorphs may be particularly susceptible to low back pain and osteoporosis.

The Mesomorph: Athletic and Muscular

Mesomorphs are nature's athletes, with hard, muscular bodies and a solid, square appearance. They're sturdily built, and their tight, short muscles and strong connective tissue give them a very upright posture, but limit their flexibility. They're medium-to-large-boned, with shoulders broader than hips, short torsos, and a well-proportioned distribution of weight.

Mesomorphs are high-energy people, with high levels of adrenaline and an efficient cardiovascular system. In general, they excel at strength and endurance activities and, men especially, tend to bulk up when they lift weights.

Depending on their diet and activity level, mesomorphs can gain or lose weight easily. Although they get into shape quickly and can eat large amounts of calories as long as they stay active, they can also lose muscle quickly and gain fat through lack of training. When they're inactive, their blood pressure and heart rate rise. That, combined with a greater concentration of fat near the middle of the body, makes them more prone to heart disease and stroke.

The Endomorph: Excess Body Fat

Endomorphs have soft, rounded, naturally curvy bodies, with excess body fat and underdeveloped muscles. Their shoulders are slightly wider than their hips, but this often goes unnoticed because they carry excess fat at their waist, buttocks, and thighs. Their posture is fairly good, and their muscles and cardiovascular system are more efficient than those of the ectomorph, though less so than the mesomorph. This gives them natural potential for strength, endurance, and flexibility. However, an overly developed digestive system and a naturally low metabolism cause them to gain weight easily and lose it slowly. The endomorph usually has a slow heart rate and low blood pressure, and can relax and fall asleep easily.

Mix and Match

You hardly ever see anyone who is a perfect ecto, meso, or endo. Most of us have traits of at least two types: Usually, we tend toward one while having traces of the others. A good pole vaulter, for instance, might be an ecto-meso, since long limbs (ectomorph) are desirable for speed and grip height, while strong upper body muscles (mesomorph) are important in levering the body over the bar.

I classify myself as an ecto-meso. Although I have the meso-morph's capacity to gain muscle and be athletic, my body's natural tendency is toward thinness.

By the way, other physical characteristics such as height, weight, or fitness level do not affect what type you are. You can be a meso, ecto, or endo of any dress size. Likewise, exercise won't change your body type. You might go from an overweight endomorph to a more slender one; from a willowy ectomorph to a more contoured one, but the changes you experience will occur relative to your own physiology.

"I think the best comment I received as a result of lifting weights was when a fellow teacher said, 'My arms flap when I write on the board, and yours never move!' My grandmother told me there was no way to keep upper arm muscles from sagging as one aged. I hate to disagree, but so far so good!"
Daphne, age 59
Aurora, IL

Body Type Self-Test

Here's a quick way to gauge your body type: Take the middle finger and thumb of one hand, and encircle the wrist of the other hand. This is a simple way of making a length-versus-width comparison of the bones in your body. This ratio gives a clue as to which category you might fall into:

fingers overlap	ectomorph
fingers touch	mesomorph
fingers don't touch	endomorph

Ectomorphs, endomorphs, and mesomorphs are like that game of rock, paper, scissors. Each can do something the others can't, so there's no better or worse type to be. And since your type was decided before you were born, your only job now is to accept and enjoy your body for its unique abilities, and learn to make the most of them.

The Mesomorph Myth

There seems to be a bias in our society in favor of the mesomorph. Most people feel that a more muscular, proportional physique is the ideal. The bias doesn't stop there, though. Studies show we actually judge people with meso physiques more favorably than others.

In one experiment, a group of psychotherapists and grad students at Midwestern State University were shown drawings of three clients' body types. Based on nothing but the outlines of the bodies, the subjects rated the clients according to various personal characteristics. Students and professionals alike all rated the mesomorphs more favorably than the others.

It's true that mesomorphs have a definite edge in most physical pursuits. However, looking beyond athletics, the other body types have edges of their own. An ectomorph's highly active nervous system may make her an exciting concert violinist. Likewise, an endomorph's slow, relaxed demeanor may make her a more approachable and reassuring presence as a school counselor.

Even in the physical realm, though, each type has its strengths. The strengths and limitations of your body type (as well as your individual goals) help determine the type of training that's right for you.

Here's a summary and some training recommendations...

Training Considerations for Each Body Type

"Since I am genetically wide hipped, by concentrating on upper body exercises I have broadened my shoulders to the point where I look much more proportioned. And it has made my everyday activities—lifting a child, pulling a wagon, pushing a swing—easier and more enjoyable."

D.P., age 49
Corpus Christi, TX

My program is designed to help everyone—no matter how you're built—develop strength, cardiovascular endurance, and flexibility. However, two people can have very different responses to the same training program. It helps to be as familiar as you can with your own body's natural tendencies, so you know how to focus your efforts and assess your progress.

Ectomorph Focus

If you're an ectomorph, you may have memories of leaving most of your elementary school classmates in the dust in the 50-yard dash. Ectomorphs are good sprinters, can become very flexible, and excel at sports involving quickness and agility. They're not gifted in the strength or endurance departments, however, and while they don't usually need to work to stay thin, they *do* need to work to stay strong.

The Role of Strength Training:

Ectomorphs need strength training to improve posture, create contour, protect joints from injury, and keep bones strong against osteoporosis.

While the ecto can improve muscle strength and endurance, the improvements may not be as great or come as fast as with the other types. An ectomorph trying to build muscle may feel at times like someone trying to grow vegetables in the desert. This is all the more reason why it's so important for ectomorphs to train, and train *consistently*.

As for other aspects of training, ectos can usually maintain flexibility with minimal effort. And because they are often high-strung, they may benefit from relaxation and stress-reduction techniques.

Mesomorph Focus

If you're a mesomorph, you've probably done well at most physical activities you've tried. If you haven't been very active up to this point, you'll probably find that your body responds quickly to training. Excess weight shouldn't be a problem as long as you stay active and eat sensibly. Because mesomorphs tend to carry fat around the center of the body, they face a greater risk of heart problems than other types if they allow their weight to climb. The right combination of strength training, cardio, and a low-fat diet will minimize this risk and keep you looking your best.

The Role of Strength Training:

Your challenge is to find a level of strength training that allows you to tone up without building more muscle than you want. Weight lifting is a must for fighting age-related muscle loss and keeping your weight down, but you may want to do it at a lower intensity (using lighter weights, according to the guidelines in Chapter 5) to avoid building unwanted bulk. Since your muscles and connective tissues tend to be tightly strung together, you'll probably need to spend extra time stretching in order to stay flexible.

THE MESOMORPH TRAP

I have an athletic body. I know I have excess fat I need to lose, but I'm afraid to strength-train because I gain muscle so easily and it's just going to make me more bulky!

Even though mesomorphs are naturally athletic, they can easily gain fat through lack of exercise and overeating. When this happens, they're often reluctant to lift weights because they're afraid more muscle will make them look bulky. I've seen many athletic-build women get caught in this trap. Your best bet, though, is a program that features strength training in combination with aerobic activity and sensible eating. While you may end up looking a little bigger in the short run, the new muscle will raise metabolic demands and help strip off the fat more quickly, revealing the shapely muscle underneath.

Training Tip: If you're a mesomorph and gain muscle easily, and you're worried about a particular area becoming too large—your legs, your triceps—then, by all means, go easy on that area. Target that muscle group with higher numbers of repetitions and less weight. But, whatever you do, don't skip working out. Even though you gain muscle easily, you can still lose it if you don't put it to use!

Endomorph Focus

If you're an endomorph, you may have memories of bringing up the rear when your classmates ran the track. Physical activity does not come easily for you, and you may find physical challenges frustrating. The main difficulty, though, is usually excess weight. Endomorphs, because of their tendency to store fat, may not *seem* to be natural athletes. But, surprisingly, they have the potential to develop strength and endurance more easily than the ectomorph.

With proper training, there's no reason an endomorph can't be toned and fit. Endos may tend to be a bit more voluptuous than other body types, but it's possible to be voluptuous *and* be in great shape!

The Role of Strength Training:

The endomorph's big challenge is her constant struggle with excess weight. Aerobic work, attention to diet, and strength training will all help. Strength training is vital, and will accomplish two things: First, it will help strengthen your joints and connective tissues to make your cardio work easier and less stressful. And second, it will help raise your metabolism so you can burn fat that much faster. Over the long run, you may want to do a little extra work on your upper body to help create a more symmetrical look.

When it comes to cardio, start with low-impact varieties to minimize stress on the joints: good choices include walking or treadmill, swimming (or aqua aerobics), low-impact aerobics, bicycling on fairly level ground, or a stationary bike with low tension.

The Art of Personalization

There's a science of exercise, but there's also an art. You start with the basic principles of training: These are well established and will work for anyone. Then, you begin to experiment, and start to notice what works best with your own body. That's the art, or the personalization, of your training. And *that* comes with experience.

Hopefully, you're starting to get a feel for your own physique and what your special challenges will be. Remember, there's nothing absolute or magical about the specific body types I've described—they just offer one way of looking at individual differences. The purpose of this chapter has been to get you *thinking* in detail about your body and its unique characteristics. Over time, and with experience, you'll learn how to make the most of them.

Now it's time to dig into the *how* of training. The next three chapters will tell you everything you need to know about the basics of weight training.

A Look Inside

How much do you really know about your body's hidden workings? Ironically, many of us know more about the operation of our computer, the ecology of our garden, or even the private lives of celebrities than we do about the miracles under our own skin!

I'm truly amazed how many of us go through life on autopilot, disconnected from ourselves in various ways: We don't know which foods don't agree with us, don't know when we're hungry and when we're full, don't recognize when we're run-down and need a break. Sometimes the disconnection is kinesthetic: I'll say to a class, "Okay, now, straighten your arms," and when I look around the room I see half the class still has their arms bent! Or sometimes it's just a simple lack of knowledge: Many well-educated people still don't know a vein from an artery, a tendon from a ligament, or even muscle from fat.

In this chapter, we'll explore some simple principles of anatomy and movement, including:

- your muscles and how they work
- body composition and the relationship of muscle to fat
- the secret to healthy bones

I promise not to make it too technical, but do try to hang in with me. I think you'll find it worthwhile. Building this foundation will not only improve your results, it will make training much more fun!

Muscle Tissue

Muscle is responsible for everything we do—in fact, it is the *essence* of doing. All actions, from a heartbeat to the contractions of childbirth—as well as, of course, moving your body through space—depend on muscle tissue. Muscles of all sizes run throughout your body and organs. Their special talent is the ability to shorten and, in so doing, exert force. There are three types of muscle:

Cardiac muscle is uniquely suited to produce the steady, lifelong contractions that keep your heart pumping.

Smooth muscle lines the walls of organs and blood vessels and produces slow, rhythmic contractions to help to push blood or other material through cavities in the body. Like cardiac muscle, it operates without your having to think about it.

Skeletal muscle is what this book is about. These are the *voluntary* muscles that attach to various points of the skeleton and enable us to move. Let's look at how this works.

Muscle Mechanics

Skeletal muscle is made up of long, cylinder-shaped **fibers**. In response to a signal from the central nervous system, tiny filaments within the fibers slide over each other like a telescope collapsing, and the muscle shortens by about one third of its length.

Muscles of all sizes are strung throughout your body to produce movements of amazing subtlety. From minute shifts of your eyes as you read this page, to sweeping motions of the limbs, muscles animate the body.

For the most part, muscles are attached to bone around **joints**, places where two bones meet and have freedom to move. Muscles connect to bone by way of tough, fibrous tissue called **tendons**. Although there are a number of different joint designs in the body, the exercises in our program will mainly involve two types:

• Hinge Joints

These operate just like the hinge on a door, allowing you to **flex** (bend) or **extend** (straighten) the joint along a single line. *Examples: elbow, knee.*

- **Ball-in-Socket Joints**

Here, a knob on the end of one bone fits into a socket or dish-shaped area on another. A ball-in-socket joint can move in any direction, although it may have greater range in some directions than in others. *Examples: hip, shoulder.*

Bones are held together at joints by ropelike straps called **ligaments**.

Muscle Pairs

As a rule, joints are operated by *pairs* of muscles, situated so they pull in opposite directions. In your arm, the biceps and triceps both cross the elbow, in front and in back respectively; one bends your arm and the other straightens it. Both muscles come into play in hammering a nail: The biceps muscle helps lift the hammer, the triceps swings it down onto the nail.

Muscles themselves always "pull" when they contract. But having them on either side of the joint lets you exert force in two directions—in other words, to push *or* pull. Anytime you jiggle a stuck door, shake an aerosol can, or nod your head, you're alternating quickly between two opposing muscles or sets of muscles.

Note: When structuring your weight training routine, it's important to strive for balanced development of opposing muscles. We'll discuss this more in Chapter 6.

Two-Joint Muscles

Some muscles span more than one joint, producing movement at both. A good example is the hamstrings—the large muscle group in the back of your legs—which run between your lower leg and pelvis, spanning both the knee and hip. When the hamstrings contract, they bend the knee *and* straighten the hip.

> "It's nice to have muscle in your body. You can hardly see mine but I can definitely feel them. After I work out, especially with weights, the muscles hurt, but it's a nice pain. I can feel the muscle itself, instead of the fat hanging around it. From my experience . . . resistance is the most effective way of building muscle and getting rid of fat."
> **Aimee, age 29**

Body Awareness Exercise: Muscle Actions

Try this: Scoot forward to the edge of the chair you're sitting in and let your right arm hang straight down at your side, palm facing forward. Reach across your body with your left hand and firmly grasp your right upper arm: fingers in front, thumb behind. Now, bend your right arm at the elbow. As you do so, you should feel the little bulge of your biceps moving inside your arm. Feel the muscle shorten as it pulls your forearm up, and lengthen as your arm goes down.

YOUR MAJOR MUSCLE GROUPS

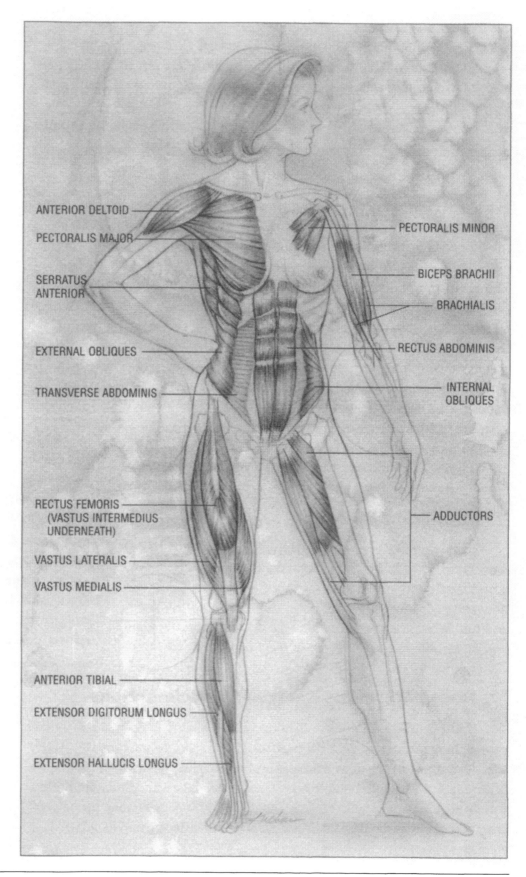

ANTERIOR DELTOID

PECTORALIS MAJOR

SERRATUS ANTERIOR

EXTERNAL OBLIQUES

TRANSVERSE ABDOMINIS

RECTUS FEMORIS (VASTUS INTERMEDIUS UNDERNEATH)

VASTUS LATERALIS

VASTUS MEDIALIS

ANTERIOR TIBIAL

EXTENSOR DIGITORUM LONGUS

EXTENSOR HALLUCIS LONGUS

PECTORALIS MINOR

BICEPS BRACHII

BRACHIALIS

RECTUS ABDOMINIS

INTERNAL OBLIQUES

ADDUCTORS

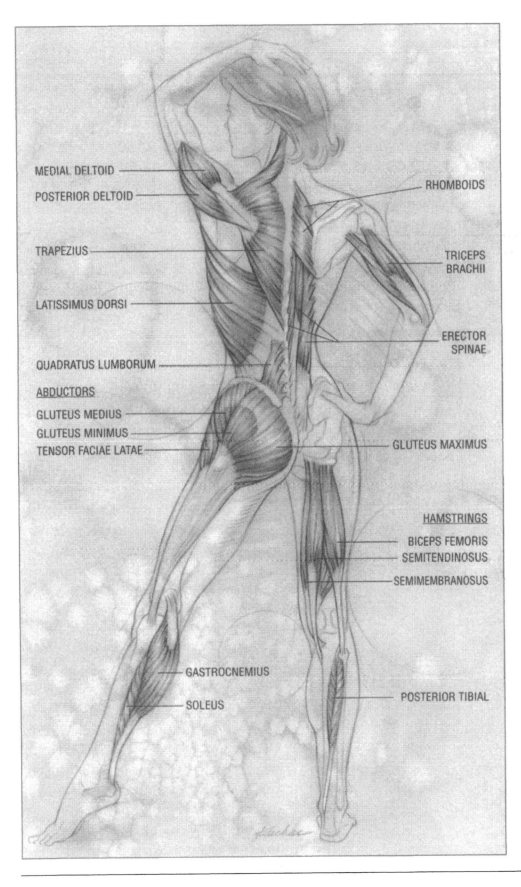

MEDIAL DELTOID

POSTERIOR DELTOID

RHOMBOIDS

TRAPEZIUS

TRICEPS BRACHII

LATISSIMUS DORSI

ERECTOR SPINAE

QUADRATUS LUMBORUM

ABDUCTORS

GLUTEUS MEDIUS

GLUTEUS MINIMUS

TENSOR FACIAE LATAE

GLUTEUS MAXIMUS

HAMSTRINGS

BICEPS FEMORIS

SEMITENDINOSUS

SEMIMEMBRANOSUS

GASTROCNEMIUS

SOLEUS

POSTERIOR TIBIAL

Two types of muscle action are occurring. On the way up, contraction of your muscle causes it to shorten. Notice, however, that as you lower your arm and the muscle lengthens, the muscle still feels tight, as if it's still contracting. That's because it is. It relaxes just enough to lose the battle with gravity, yet it keeps pulling to keep the motion under control. Think of a crane lowering a steel girder into place.

These two actions have technical-sounding names that are worth knowing. The contraction that raises your arm is called the **concentric** contraction, while the smaller contraction that slows the arm's descent is called the **eccentric** contraction. These terms will come up again when we talk about exercise technique.

There's one other type of muscle action, called an **isometric** contraction, in which the muscle tenses, but no movement occurs. To experience this, place one fist in the palm of the other hand and press them together.

Degree of Contraction

Somehow, your muscles have to be able to control the amount of tension they generate, to make sure it's appropriate for the task at hand. Imagine if they didn't—you might try to pick up a glass of water and find yourself hurling it to the ceiling!

To provide for this, the fibers of each muscle are divided into a number of parcels called **motor units,** each of which is triggered individually. The more strength you need at a given moment, the more motor units are recruited to fire—up to a point, that is, and that point depends on your level of conditioning. If you're out of shape, only a small percentage of your available muscle units are likely to be recruited. Most of the strength gains you get from weight training—about 80 percent, in fact— actually come from your nerves "learning" to be more efficient at enlisting dormant fibers. That's why, in the early stages of training, you can double, or even triple your strength in a relatively short time without increasing the size of your muscles much at all.

Properties of Muscle: Strength, Endurance, and Tone

There are two things your muscles are asked to do in everyday life. One is to create a lot of force for a moment—say, to lift that five-gallon water bottle onto the cooler without dropping it and flooding the kitchen. The other is to exert force repeatedly or steadily over time: Imagine holding your arms over your head while pruning a hedge.

The force a muscle can generate in a momentary exertion defines its **strength.** The ability to *sustain* a contraction, or contract repeatedly many times, is called **endurance**. Strength and endurance are two different features of muscle performance, but they both come into play constantly during daily activity.

Training for strength requires that you lift a relatively large amount of weight a few times until the muscle tires. Because a muscle's strength relates in part to its size, training for strength will cause slight increases in size as well. As I said a moment ago, though, most of your strength gains will come from neurological changes that allow you to lift more efficiently.

Training for endurance, on the other hand, requires that you lift relatively lighter weights, and lift them more times. This teaches your muscles to postpone fatigue by developing more efficient ways to obtain oxygen and nutrients and dispose of waste products.

> The word "muscle" comes from the Latin *musculus*, which means "little mouse"— named for the shape of certain muscles when they move under the skin.

A third property of muscle, **tone**, refers to the firmness of the muscle at rest. Even when you're sleeping, muscles remain slightly tensed. If you're out of shape, their level of resting contraction is low and the muscles appear loose and mushy. As you become more fit, they develop greater resting tension and firmness. Both strength and endurance training will improve your muscle tone.

Body Composition: Muscle vs. Fat

For many people, the only indication they have of changes taking place in their body is the bathroom scale. Gained a pound . . . lost a pound . . . back at my usual weight—and so on. We imagine that the only thing that's happening inside are small changes in the amount of fat we're storing.

If fat were the only variable, a glance at the scale *would* tell the story. But, in fact, everything is changing: fat, muscle, water, possibly even bone. That's why the important question isn't "What's my weight?" but "What's my weight *composed* of?"

Body composition—especially the proportions of fat and muscle—is the measure of your fitness. Although our basic build and height don't change much, body composition can fluctuate quite a bit.

The Energy Equation

LIGHT MEAT, DARK MEAT

How do your muscles meet the demand for strength versus endurance? Nature has designed specialized muscle fibers for each job. If you've ever made a meal of chicken or duck, you've noticed the light and dark meat that distinguishes these two types of muscle.

Fast twitch (white muscle) fibers are designed for strength. They're able to produce large amounts of tension for a short time, but they tire easily and are best suited to activities such as sprinting, jumping, or strength training.

Slow twitch (red muscle) fibers are designed for endurance. They produce smaller amounts of force that can be sustained over time. They come into play during aerobic activity. (Interestingly, ducks have red breast meat, enabling them to fly long distances, whereas chickens' white breast meat keeps them essentially grounded.)

Large muscles in your body may contain over a thousand fibers of each type. Some smaller muscles are more specialized. In the calf, for instance, there are two muscles: The *soleus*, mostly slow twitch, provides the necessary endurance for hours of standing or walking, while the *gastrocnemius*, mostly fast twitch, is useful for sprinting and jumping.

The exact proportion of fast and slow fibers in your body is part of your unique genetic makeup and influences whether you'll do better at strength or endurance activities.

A layer of fat blankets the muscle on your body. Perhaps because of this proximity, the relationship between muscle and fat can be confusing. They're completely separate and distinct tissues, yet there *is* a connection. Muscle and fat are key players in the big energy exchange known as your body's **metabolism**.

As I said earlier, metabolism refers to the conversion of energy within your body. Food goes in, and your body converts it to the energy it needs to support life. Anything left over after all the metabolic needs are met is stored as fat.

Muscle and fat, therefore, represent the two sides of the energy coin: Muscle is the engine, fat is the fuel. Fat tissue stores energy; muscle tissue expends it, during activity and at rest. This is why lean muscle mass and fat are often changing in opposite directions. Here's the standard profile:

• Your lean muscle naturally declines with age.

An inactive woman begins losing about one-half pound of muscle every year after age 35.

• Your metabolism slows.

Each pound of muscle you lose deprives you of some of your calorie-burning engine power.

• You store more fat.

With each passing year, you lose more muscle, and convert more excess calories to fat. Assuming your eating habits remain the same, fat will accumulate faster and faster as time goes on.

Net result: You've traded muscle for fat. Interestingly, the scale may not show much change in weight, but the actual makeup of your body has changed drastically. Fat is less dense than muscle, so the fat you've gained takes up more space than the muscle you've lost. You may weigh about the same, but your clothes have gotten tighter.

Turning Back the Clock

Fortunately, this process works in reverse, too. Because the resting energy needs of muscle tissue are greater than those of fat, putting extra muscle on your frame is like turning on all the lights and appliances in your house: Suddenly you're using more energy all the time.

In a study done at Tufts University, 12 men and women, age 56 to 80, spent 12 weeks resistance training. They all ate enough to maintain the weight they started with—on the scale, that is. Yet while their weight held steady, their body composition shifted: Fat mass dropped as lean mass rose. The new muscle boosted their body's energy demands by about 15 percent. Since they were on a maintenance diet, the extra fuel needed to meet the higher energy demand had to come from their fat stores. The study concluded that resistance training is an effective way to raise energy requirements and decrease body fat in healthy older people. What worked for them will work for you.

Through resistance training, you may find yourself dropping several dress sizes even though your weight remains about the same—and you'll look trimmer, simply because your new muscle takes up less space than fat.

How Much Fat Is Ideal?

In a woman's body, fat should ideally represent about 22 to 25 percent of total body weight. If yours is higher, though, you're not alone: American women commonly have body fat in the 35 to 40 percent range. This suggests two things: first, that the "ideal" percentage may vary a bit from

> *"In just a few weeks [of strength training], my overall strength increased so much that I had to increase the poundage of the weights. Shortly afterward, I noticed the cellulite on the back of my legs was diminishing—something I had not been able to accomplish when doing only aerobics. Finally, at age 32, I have reached a healthy weight and am comfortable with my size."*
> **Tracy**
> **Greensburg, PA**

person to person; and second, that most of us could stand to lose a little! There are various ways to measure your body fat. The most accurate—hydrostatic measuring—is rather costly and troublesome. I recommend investing in an inexpensive pair of plastic skinfold calipers. These are easy to use and provide an acceptable degree of accuracy.

Do you believe that a lean body composition is within your grasp? There's no doubt about it. Another study compared female athletes to sedentary women from age 18 to 69 and found that the *athletic* 69-year-olds had the same body fat percentage as the athletic 18-year-olds. I rest my case!

Problem Areas and Spot Reducing

We've been talking about fat tissue in general, but what about *specific* problem areas? First of all, what makes one area a problem? Simply that it's the first place fat goes—the spot that looks bad even when the rest of you is looking pretty good. And *because* it's the first place fat goes, it's also the last place it leaves—the hardest place to slim down.

Truth is, everyone is born with a certain distribution of fat cells, determined by her genes. Unless the fat is evenly distributed, there will always be some areas that accumulate it first and stubbornly retain it.

Can I reduce my problem areas by targeting them with weight training?

You *can* reduce, but you *can't* target.

As we've said, weight training builds muscle. Having additional muscle throughout your body will raise your metabolism and burn calories faster. In this way, weight training helps remove fat *generally*. However, the idea of being able to "spot-reduce" fat by targeting the muscles in a specific area is, once and for all, a myth! Devoting more work to your triceps in particular will build the triceps muscle, but won't have any specific effect on the fat in your arms.

Remember, muscle and fat are two completely distinct tissues. Even though they appear side by side throughout the body, a muscle has no direct effect on the fat that happens to lie next to it.

What about cellulite?

Practically speaking, cellulite is just ordinary fat that has started to bulge through openings in the layer of connective tissue that covers it, creating a dimpling of the skin. It's similar to what happens when you sit in a lawn chair and your skin bulges through the holes. Although topical treatments to improve the *appearance* of cellulite are being studied, reducing the fat layer through diet and exercise is still the safest and most long-lasting solution.

The Hard Truth About Bones

Bones are the hardest of all living tissues, but they're far from invulnerable. As most of us know by now, we lose bone density as we age; most of us have seen the effects of this change in our mothers and grandmothers. In time, loss of bone causes our skeleton to shrink and become more fragile. In the U.S. alone, bone loss accounts for over one million fractures every year in people over 50.

What exactly is bone density?

Bone is made up of a sturdy meshwork of fibers and cells, impregnated with minerals—specifically calcium. Healthy bone tissue is strong and dense like a piece of hardwood.

Bone density reaches its peak sometime around age 30 or 35, after which it starts to decline by about .5 percent a year. The rate of loss may climb to 1 to 2 percent a year during the first decade after menopause. In this way, a woman can easily lose up to 30 percent of her bone mass by the time she turns 60—unless she takes steps to retain it.

Fortunately, there's a lot that can be done to slow, or even reverse, the natural rate of bone loss—and weight lifting is turning out to play a powerful role. In a recent study, researchers at Tufts University compared postmenopausal women on a strength training program to a second group who didn't exercise. They found that, while the sedentary control group lost 2 percent of their bone density over the course of a year, the weight lifters actually *gained* 1 percent during the same period!

What causes bone loss?

Your bone tissue depends on several things to replenish itself and remain strong. These include proper nutrients to provide the building material of bone, and adequate levels of hormones and physical activity to stimulate growth.

• Calcium depletion:

Your bones are made of calcium and other minerals and act as a calcium storehouse, supplying the mineral where it's needed for a variety of processes. As long as the supply is replenished, there's no problem. But if you're not getting enough calcium in your diet, the stores in the bone remain depleted. This is why it's important for many women to take supplemental calcium, as well as other minerals. Researchers are still investigating ideal dosages; consult with your doctor for specific recommendations.

• *Changes in hormone levels:*

Estrogen stimulates the cells responsible for bone growth; decreased levels of estrogen after menopause allow bone loss to accelerate. Your doctor can help you determine if hormone replacement therapy is appropriate for you.

• *Lack of physical activity:*

As I said earlier, your bones rely on the physical stress of exercise—specifically, of weight-bearing activity—to stimulate them to remain strong. A vivid example came when scientists discovered that astronauts in a weightless environment on the Mir space station were losing bone mass at a rate of *up to 1 percent a month.* At that rate, voyagers to Mars would be suffering from osteoporosis before they ever got there! Clearly, load-bearing exercise is vital for long-term skeletal health.

> I know the idea of bone loss sounds grim, but consider it a wake-up call. The years before and surrounding menopause are the prime time to take the steps that can prevent osteoporosis!

Osteoporosis

Osteoporosis affects more than 20 million women, most of them over 45. Over time, calcium depletion in the bones causes them to become brittle and porous. Sadly, the first warning many women get that they've reached this point is a fracture of the hip or spine, often from a stress as minor as a sudden movement. Unfortunately, by this point, the condition is well advanced and difficult, if not impossible, to treat with much success.

Osteoporosis affects women at a rate of about four to one over men, for several reasons:

- Being generally smaller, women have less bone to lose.
- Men are protected by their level of testosterone, which stimulates bone growth.
- Women are more apt to follow restrictive diets that deprive them of necessary nutrients.
- Women, until recently, haven't participated as much in the types of load-bearing and strength training activities that can help maintain healthy bone.

The best remedy is always prevention. Although aerobic training can help—even walking as little as one mile a day can improve bone density— we're discovering that resistance training can complete the picture by addressing areas of the body not affected by typical weight-bearing activities. Dozens of studies in recent years have shown that resistance training can improve bone density, and that the combination of nutritional therapy (specifically calcium and vitamin D supplementation) and weight training is more effective than a strictly nutritional approach.

> "I am postmenopausal and have a small frame. My concern is loss of bone density. I have elected not to take HRT. I prefer to rely on proper diet and exercise with an emphasis on weight bearing exercises to help prevent bone loss. So far, it seems to be working. My bone density at this point is still in the normal range."
> **Maryellen, age 58**

Where bone loss is more advanced, hormone replacement therapy (HRT) can be beneficial, especially when taken in conjunction with exercise, but HRT is likely to produce side effects. New drugs are constantly being tested, so talk with your doctor about possible side effects of HRT, and ask what other options are available.

Strength training, more than drug or nutritional therapy, carries the additional benefits of improving strength and increasing balance and muscle mass, thereby addressing the whole complex of factors that can limit physical activity and increase the risk of osteoporosis.

Now that we've spent a little time looking at the body's physical structure, you should have a much better sense of what strength training will do for you. In the next chapter, we'll continue laying the groundwork for our program by exploring the basic principles of resistance training.

Chapter 5

Exercise Basics

Weight lifting is a simple concept: You take a weight, and you make it go up and down. Of course, there are rules to help you do it safely and efficiently. But there really isn't anything terribly mysterious about it. It's a formalized version of something we do every day.

I've spoken with so many women who claim they're afraid to weight-train. "I don't want to be muscular!" they say. Then, all of a sudden, they deliver a 9-pound baby, who, within about two months, weighs 15 pounds. Two months later that's doubled—now they're carrying around, on that one arm, *a 30-pound baby.* I look at these women and say: "I hate to break it to you, but you're weight-training!"

Sure, there's a little more to a formal weight training program. There's a more carefully controlled structure, more variety of exercise to reach all muscle groups, scheduled rest periods, and careful attention to form in order to prevent injury. In a real training program, the weights don't get heavier before you're ready for it—and they don't squirm in your arms! Still, a woman who's hefting a 30-pound baby all day has no reason to object to the *idea* of lifting weights, since, whether she knows it or not, she's already putting the principle into practice! She would have everything to gain from a formal weight training program—it would simply help build *extra* strength that would make her life easier.

In the next two chapters, we're going to go through the basic principles of weight training. There are many different training systems out there, but they all boil down to the same elements of *resistance, overload, sets, reps,* and a *schedule* for working out. First, we'll talk about the factors that relate to the exercises themselves. Then, we'll discuss your routine as a whole.

Resistance

In the last chapter, we saw how the muscle and joint systems in your body work. One of the most basic principles of weight training is that it provides something for your muscles to work *against*. That something is called **resistance**.

There are various ways to create resistance. The most familiar are free weights, such as dumbbells or barbells. Other resistance devices include weight machines and elastic bands. Of course, your own body weight can provide resistance—for example, when doing push-ups or pull-ups. Our program will mainly employ dumbbells and body weight, since these are the most versatile tools for home use. However, I'll also provide exercises that involve other types of equipment, in case you have access to a gym and prefer to train there.

Range of Motion

Some muscle contractions produce movement, while others don't. Ever try to slide open a window that's been painted shut? You stand there, pushing for all you're worth, but nothing budges. As I mentioned earlier, this is called an isometric contraction. Now imagine throwing a ball or picking up a weight. Here the tensing of the muscles causes movement of joints and limbs. This is called a **dynamic,** or **isotonic,** contraction. Most of the exercises in our program involve dynamic contraction of the target muscles.

In real-life situations (as well as in weight lifting), dynamic contractions of one muscle or muscle group are often assisted by the isometric contractions of other muscles (usually of the trunk or legs) acting to stabilize the body. That's why I've included one group of exercises that specifically focuses on the stabilizing function of these muscles and uses mostly isometric contraction to do so. That said, though, *most* of the exercises we'll be doing involve dynamic contraction and some range of motion.

In exercises involving dynamic contraction (and again, that's most of them), it's important to move the muscle through the full range of motion called for in the exercise descriptions. The more diligent you are about training through the muscle's full range—thereby mimicking the motions in everyday life—the more the strength you build will carry over to daily tasks.

> Work the muscles through the full range of motion indicated in the descriptions in the exercise section.

Overload

There you are, just getting used to the idea that a little extra muscle could be a good thing, and I hit you with a scary-sounding word like **overload!** But it really isn't that scary. Overloading just means that if you want to stimulate your muscles to grow, you have to ask them to do more than they're accustomed to.

If you've ever done aerobics, you've already experienced the principle of overload. In aerobics, overloading is often accomplished by increasing *duration*. You force your body to exercise for longer and longer periods of time, thereby burning calories, strengthening your heart, and building muscular endurance.

In weight training, the basic components of overload are the *amount of weight* you lift, and *how many times* you lift it. Here, the idea is to work the muscle to the point of fatigue very quickly—within about 30 to 90 seconds. Pushing the muscle to fatigue is also called "working to failure." Don't let the idea of pushing your muscles to fatigue, or failure, scare you. This is the key to muscle growth: When the muscle "fails," you've succeeded!

Progression

Over time, you'll become stronger, and the resistance that once provided an overload won't be an overload any longer. That's why overload must be **progressive**. The only way to keep building your strength is to keep challenging your muscles to do more.

> "I don't think I will ever exercise again without weights. Using weights makes you feel like you are accomplishing more each time you exercise."
> **Pamela, age 48**
> **Ellenwood, GA**

This is why weights are so useful. Although you can do a lot with body weight exercises (especially if you know how to make adjustments to vary the resistance), they're often apt to be too easy or too hard. Once you reach a certain level of strength, for instance, it's very hard to train your legs using only body weight. With weights, you can gradually increase the resistance in small, precise increments.

Progression can be achieved by adding more weight, more sets, or more exercises. Another way is by working out more frequently—say, three times a week instead of twice. Progression can also be accomplished through greater mental focus: Sometimes just becoming more experienced and adept at doing the exercises allows you to pour on more steam without actually changing your routine.

Sets and Reps

When you pick up a weight and prepare to do an exercise, you'll have a specific goal in mind—a certain number of sets and reps called for in the routine. A **rep** is a *repetition,* meaning a single contraction and release. A rep has a positive, or concentric, phase, in which you're contracting the muscle, and a negative, or eccentric, phase, in which you relax and allow the weight to return to the starting position.

A **set** is a certain number of reps done one after another without rest. Typically, a routine would call for anywhere from one to three sets of a given exercise. Research shows, however, that *most* of the training effect—upward of 80 percent—occurs during the first set (assuming you make an all-out effort), especially if you're just starting to train. This means you can get very nearly the same results in about half the time by doing single sets of most exercises.

Low Reps vs. High Reps

Different rep ranges produce slightly different results. Initially, my program will call for higher ranges of up to 20 reps per set. Higher reps allow you to use less weight; this reduces your risk of injury and helps you ease gently into the program, while still producing great results.

Once you've developed some basic strength in your muscles, tendons, and ligaments from several weeks of high-rep training, you'll be able to do heavier sets of fewer reps. People looking for maximum gains in muscle size generally train in the 6 to 8 rep range. For our purposes, though, training in the 8 to 12 range will be enough to produce the *slight* increases in muscle size necessary to create shape and contour, while also improving strength and tone.

Higher reps, in the 15 to 20 rep range, will increase strength, endurance, and tone, but will not significantly change the muscles' size. This means that if you're lifting weights to develop muscle contour, you should train using lower reps with more weight; whereas if you're worried about increasing muscle size but still want to develop some tone and strength, you should work with lighter weights at higher reps.

How Much Weight Should I Lift?

Knowing how much weight to use is easy, because it's determined by the rep and set goals specified in the routine. In each case, you'll use an amount of weight you can just *barely* lift the required number of times and still maintain proper form. For example, a typical rep goal might be 10 to 12 reps. With a little experimenting, you'd choose a weight that causes your muscles to give out somewhere in that 10 to 12 rep range. Ideally, you'd be able to do the 10th, 11th, or 12th rep with proper form, yet feel like you couldn't go any further without a rest.

GOAL: 10–12 REPS			
Reps:	1–6	7–9	10–12
Should feel:	Moderately heavy	Difficult	The limit of what you can do and still maintain good form

Speed of Reps: Slow and Steady

The speed of reps is a big factor in creating an overload. EMG (electromyographic) studies (which record electrical activity in a muscle during exertion) show that muscles work hardest when you lift at a slow, controlled pace. For best results, try to make each rep last about 4 to 7 seconds, or a count of 2 to 3 seconds in each direction. This will prevent you from cheating by using momentum to make the lift easier.

REP GUIDELINES

- Low rep/high resistance training is the most efficient way to develop strength, tone, and size.
- Higher rep/lower resistance work will develop some strength, muscular endurance, and tone, but won't maximize the muscles' size.
- Don't lift more than you can and still maintain proper form.
- Lift slowly and with control: about 2 to 3 seconds in each direction.

Pace: Keep It Moving!

If you're doing more than one set of an exercise, you need to give your muscle a little time to recover between sets. For best results, these breaks should be brief. Try to keep rest between sets to no more than 30 to 45 seconds. Between exercises, as well, some time will naturally elapse while you move to the next position—just don't let it stretch out too long. If you stop for a conversation between each set or exercise, you're allowing too much time for the muscles to recover, and you probably won't reach the level of fatigue necessary for muscle growth. In general, try to keep all rest periods under 45 seconds.

PACE GUIDELINE

Limit rest periods between sets to 30 to 45 seconds.

Focus on Form!

"I thought that if you lifted weights you would get those huge muscles. I didn't know that with lighter weights and more repetition a person could just get a nicely toned figure and not look like the Hulk. I love the way [weight training] tones and sculpts the arms, back, chest, butt, and legs. I've gained self-confidence—and a healthy sex life!"

Dawn, age 21
Norfolk, VA

The issue of proper exercise form should be foremost in your mind every time you work out. Exercising with good form can make the difference between fast, safe, great-looking results, and frustration—sometimes even injury.

Each exercise in this program is described in detail in the exercise section. Be sure to read the descriptions carefully. Don't just fall into doing the movement in any old way, simply because you're familiar with the exercise. Sweat the details!

What is good form?

In simple terms, good form means *proper alignment of your body in relation to the resistance.* For each exercise you do, there will be a precise way to position your body that will best align the system of muscles and joints with the resistance, enabling you to work most efficiently. Strike that pose and you'll get faster results, with the least waste of effort or risk of injury.

How to Guarantee Good Form

If this sounds complicated, don't worry. I'm not suggesting you have to master all the principles of physics just to lift weights! Just know that the fine points of form do make a difference—in fact, they can make *all* the difference. There are two things you can do to ensure good form:

• *Study the instructions carefully and keep checking yourself.*

Those mirrors in the gym aren't there just for vanity. Like the mirrors in a ballet studio, they're there to help you perfect your form. If you're working at home, work in front of a mirror if possible.

• *Know which muscle you're working, where it's located, and what it does.*

In the exercise section, I'll note the location of each muscle or muscle group we train. If possible, use your free hand to feel the muscles while they're working. That way you can gauge how changes in position affect the tension of the muscle.

Biceps Curl with proper form.

Wrong! Biceps Curl with poor form: body is way out of alignment! This reduces the exercise's effectiveness and can lead to injury.

Breathe!

When I was in labor delivering my first daughter, I used some of the breathing techniques I'd learned in yoga. People in the delivery room were asking me, "What kind of breathing is that you're doing? You seem so relaxed!" I'm a big believer in using breath to manage my stress level and state of mind.

When I'm exercising, breathing is my focal point. I match the breath to the movement, exhaling as I exert, inhaling on the release. Like the quick expansion of air that moves a piston, the exhale drives the motion. Expend the energy (the breath), then pull the energy back in and replenish. *Out goes the bad air, in comes the good!*

At times while lifting, you might catch yourself holding your breath. When you notice this happening, exhale and bring your breathing back into step with your motion. Holding your breath is not only less effective, it can raise your blood pressure and possibly damage small blood vessels. When you develop a smooth breathing rhythm, it fuels your workout and keeps you feeling energized.

Try exhaling steadily as you lift, and inhale as you release. If you need to breathe more frequently, by all means do so. Just try to make your breathing an integral part of the exercise.

> "At first I dreaded weight lifting days because I didn't know what I was doing. Then I learned the correct way to do each exercise and what body parts they were for. I've noticed not only overall toning, but increased strength and energy to carry out normal daily tasks. Now instead of dreading the weight lifting days, I look forward to them and almost crave them."
>
> Lisa Hepworth, age 27
> Pocatello, ID

Isolation and Functional Strength

One of the fun things about weight training is that it lets you zero in on a specific muscle and work it in **isolation**. If you want to sculpt and contour a special area of your body, isolation exercises are the most efficient way.

But weight lifting offers another, more important benefit called **functional strength.** As the name suggests, this is strength that helps you *function* better by making all your daily tasks seem easier. Functional strength is central to good health and enjoyment of life. However, isolation exercises aren't the way to build it. Here's why:

In real life, muscles rarely work alone. Most everyday moves are complex enough to require a coordinated effort from several muscles. Picture yourself performing some common motions: opening a window, climbing stairs, lifting your child. We hardly ever bend or extend at the elbow without some movement at the shoulder as well. And how often when walking, climbing, or lifting do you bend your leg at the hip, without some bend occurring at the knee? Almost always, there are several muscles at work, moving more than one joint.

The best way to train your muscles to handle these complex everyday movements is with exercises that make the same demands. Functional strength exercises involve multiple joints and teach all the muscles involved to work together more efficiently. Some, like the Face-Down Plank, involve little or no motion, instead using isometric contractions to develop stability and balance. In general, exercises that involve multiple joints and make stabilizing demands create a more useful, practical kind of strength than you'd get if you tried to train the same muscles in isolation.

> Both isolation and functional strength exercises have their place, and our program will include both.

Muscle Soreness and Pain

I think one thing about weight lifting that puts women off is watching the grimacing and groaning that *men* do when they lift. Well, I won't lie to you, making that weight go up and down *is* an effort—it's supposed to be! But is it supposed to be painful?

The answer is no, it shouldn't be *painful*—but we need to define our terms.

Muscular effort produces a sensation known as "the burn." It's caused by a metabolic by-product, **lactic acid,** that accumulates in the muscle as you approach the point of failure. It's a strange feeling, and I'll admit at first I hated it. I'd be doing Leg Extensions, for instance, and at about the fifth rep I'd start to feel as if my legs were on fire. Well, I don't know when the switch happened, but now I love that sensation. It's like a big neon sign lighting up spelling "Success!"

The burn that accompanies muscular fatigue is very different from the acute stab of pain that signals strain or injury. Sharp or severe pain is never good. A sensation of heat, though, is normal and tells you that you've succeeded in overloading the muscle. Even so, I recommend moderation: It's not necessary to push every exercise into the realm of smoldering agony. And, again, *never* push your muscles to do more reps than you can do with good form.

Soreness After a Workout

I'm sure you've heard people say: "I'm sore in muscles I didn't even know I had!" Well, it does happen. Don't be surprised if, after your first few workouts, you go to climb a staircase one day and discover that some-one has replaced your leg muscles with overdone linguini. Whenever you push your training to a new level, you're apt to feel some soreness and weakness afterward. This is especially true if you're starting to weight-train for the first time. The soreness is caused by microscopic tears and inflam-mation that are a common side effect of overloading the muscles. There are several things you can do to minimize it:

- Begin your training easily and progress gradually.
- Don't push every exercise into the "burning" range.
- Allow a muscle group at least 48 hours rest between workouts.
- Always stop immediately if you feel acute pain.

The famous "no pain, no gain" slogan is a macho misnomer. Building muscle will involve new physical sensations that may be a little uncomfort-able at first. But if it's truly painful, something's wrong.

Enjoy the Experience!

I'm convinced that a familiarity with, and understanding of, the physi-cal sensations associated with weight lifting is key to success. You can read about something all day long, but it's when you finally get out of your head and into the experience that it comes alive and becomes part of you. That's also when it becomes fun! Being able to monitor and reflect on your physical experience enables you to refine the process. Eventually, you'll be able to know when it's right because it *feels* right.

In Chapter 8, I'll talk more about how you can use the physical sensa-tion of weight lifting as a motivational tool. Now, let's continue our ground-work with a look at the principles behind putting together a good weight training routine.

Chapter 6

Your Routine

So often, people make it harder on themselves when they try to work out because they don't start with a clear plan. They'll throw exercises together in a haphazard way, overdoing some things and neglecting others. This is a formula for frustration. The truth is, how you put exercises *together* is just as important as the exercises themselves. Without a properly structured routine, your efforts just won't add up to the results you want.

The Hallmarks of a Good Routine

What exactly is a **routine?** Your routine is the framework, or system, that brings all the elements of your workout together, focusing them on the goal you're trying to achieve. A good routine should address the following points:

- *Selection:* Choosing a well-balanced assortment of exercises.
- *Sequence:* Arranging the exercises in an order that will produce the greatest results.
- *Progression:* Gradually raising the intensity.

- *Schedule:* Working out often enough to get results without over-doing it.
- *Rest:* Allowing your muscles adequate time to recover between workouts.
- *Variety:* Finding new ways to challenge your muscles and brain over time.

My *Lift Weights to Lose Weight* program does the planning for you. The routines included in this book are "prepackaged," according to the guidelines in this chapter. The first 12 weeks of your training are mapped out in detail in the Training Log; all you have to do is follow the instructions and you're guaranteed great results.

Nevertheless, I encourage you to read on and absorb some of the principles on which the program is based. That way, if you want to customize your routine in any way, you're equipped to do so. Remember, it's when you begin to understand the principles of training for yourself that it becomes most effective—and fun!

Selection: How Many Exercises Should I Do?

The key in selecting exercises is *coverage*. In the early stages of training, you don't need to do multiple exercises for each body part. A routine consisting of 8 to 10 exercises is enough to cover all the basic muscle groups and create a solid strength base for further work. In the exercise section in Chapter 10, you'll find a wide assortment of exercises, arranged by body part. If you want to put together your own routine—for variety, or to accommodate certain equipment limitations—simply choose 8 to 10 exercises, one from each body part category.

Keeping It Balanced

In the heat of your workout, you might be tempted to concentrate on a few favorite exercises or body parts while neglecting others. Sometimes, people just focus on the areas of their body that seem to respond the best. This can cause strength imbalances and may lead to injury.

As you may remember from Chapter 4, joints are operated by pairs of *opposing muscles* that pull the moving end of the joint back and forth. A simple joint like the elbow, which moves in only two directions, has a single pair of muscles (the biceps and triceps) that tug against each other.

Ball-in-socket joints like the hip have several pairs of opposing muscles that give them their full range of motion. These opposing muscles help to stabilize the joint.

It's important to maintain a balance of strength between opposing muscles. Otherwise, the joint becomes unstable and more easily injured. To assure balanced development and strength, a good training routine should devote equal effort to building all opposing muscle group pairs. Balanced development is also important for good posture, and helps create a more well-proportioned, symmetrical physique.

The routines in my program provide a full range of exercises to guarantee a healthy balance of strength of opposing muscles.

Sequence: Is Order Important?

Does it really matter what order you do the exercises in? If you want the maximum return on your time, the answer's yes. The right order will help *all* the muscles get a fair and equal workout. The reason has to do with how muscles interrelate, a principle called **interdependency**.

Muscle Interdependency

Individual muscles rarely act alone. Especially in real-life situations, they're always cooperating to get things done. Even in the gym, where you're doing your best to target a single muscle, other muscles always get into the act—either to assist with the motion or simply as stabilizers, working to hold your body in place.

Generally speaking, the muscles near the center of the body, such as your chest, back, and hip muscles, are the ones most likely to depend on help from outlying muscles of the arms and legs. For example, push-ups are a common chest exercise. But could you do a push-up without using your arms? Of course not! In most common exercises involving free weights or body weight, your chest muscles depend on your shoulders and arms to help them get a good workout.

Help Your Muscles Help Each Other

To make sure *all* the muscles get a thorough workout, we have to take their interdependent relationships into account. We've just mentioned how certain chest exercises involve arm and shoulder muscles as well. If

"At first I wasn't sure about weights. I thought it might be hard. Within 3 months I could see a difference. Not only did the pounds melt off, but it also defined the shape of my whole body. My energy level went sky high. Friends I hadn't seen in over six months couldn't believe how great I looked."
T.J., age 31
Garden City, MI

you started your workout by working your arms to a frazzle, they wouldn't be much help when you tried to do chest exercises. Your chest muscles would never get a full workout. The key to finding a good exercise order is to figure out which exercises rely most heavily on helping muscles and do those first, while the helping muscles are still fresh. This way, no muscle becomes a weak link in the effort to overload the others. The rule of thumb concerning exercise order is:

Work from the center of the body outward.

Following this rule, you'd work hips and buttocks before working thighs, calves, and shins. Likewise, you'd work chest and back before tiring out your shoulders and arms.

By the way, this system leaves plenty of room for variety. For instance, it doesn't matter whether you start with upper or lower body. Opposing muscles, such as biceps and triceps, are interchangeable, and abs exercises may be done before or after the other muscle groups.

Progression: Increase the Intensity

As we learned in the last chapter, the resistance needed to overload your muscles and stimulate them to grow must be progressive—it must increase as the muscles become stronger.

My program begins with a 4-week introductory phase designed to gently ease your body into weight training. In that first phase, we'll be working in a high-rep range of 18 to 20 reps, enabling you to use relatively light weights. This will gradually strengthen your tendons and ligaments, and slowly bring your muscles to life. The introductory phase is a learning period for your muscles. During this time, pushing the muscle to the point of fatigue is not as important as developing good technique.

Once you've developed a feel for the exercises and gained a basic level of strength in your muscles and joints, we'll begin to build on that foundation. In the second and third blocks of the program, we'll slowly lower the target rep ranges to allow you to use a little more weight. In addition, we'll keep changing the exercises and sequence to vary the stresses and urge your muscles into the realm of maximum results.

Schedule: What's My Time Commitment?

When you're first starting out, you can get good results training just 2 days a week. Because your muscles are experiencing something new, a little effort translates into big returns. Over time—after the first 3 or 4 months—your schedule will depend on your goals: If you want to continue to build strength, you'll probably need to increase to 3 or 4 workouts a week; however, you can *maintain* strength gains quite effectively with just 2 workouts a week.

The Training Log in Chapter 10 provides space for the 2 required workouts each week, plus an extra space for an optional 3rd workout.

Rest: As Important as Training Itself!

I have women say to me, "Kathy, I love training my legs so much I do it every day—sometimes *twice* a day!" Whoa, wait a minute! I love your enthusiasm, but it's possible to get too much of a good thing.

To grow stronger, your muscles need rest just as much as they need training: The two go hand in hand. The fact is, the beneficial changes to your muscles don't happen *during* your workout, they happen while your muscles are resting. It's vital to give muscles at least 48 hours of downtime between weight training workouts.

Does that mean I can't strength train two days in a row?

No, it just means you shouldn't work the *same muscle group* two days in a row. This still leaves you free to structure your time in many different ways. Frankly, my first phase routine is so short that most people will probably work their whole body on the same day. Still, if you want to split it up, you can: In the first block of the program, for instance, instead of doing two 20-minute workouts a week, you can do four 10-minute workouts. In this way, you can work out 2 days in a row by alternating body parts. For example:

"Before the end of the first week I began to feel like I had something to look forward to, something for me. My energy began to peak again and my muscles began to feel a bit more firm. Success, for me, has not come in pounds and inches lost; my success goes much deeper. I am getting myself back emotionally and mentally, with the added benefit of physical improvement as well."
Jennifer
Cool, CA

MON	**WED**
Full Body	Full Body
(20 minutes)	(20 minutes)

—or—

MON	**TUES**	**THURS**	**FRI**
Upper Body	Lower Body	Upper Body	Lower Body
(10 minutes)	(10 minutes)	(10 minutes)	(10 minutes)

With either schedule, you're still following the basic rule that each muscle gets a minimum of 48 hours between workouts.

Variety: Keeping It Fresh

Varying your workout is the key to avoiding boredom and staleness. At first, your muscles will be adjusting to the strange new experience of weight training and will benefit from a consistent routine. Over time, though, a little variety will help keep your training fresh and fun. Finding ways to vary your weight training routine (and your overall fitness activity as well) will improve your results, decrease your risk of injury from overuse, and keep your enthusiasm high. There are lots of ways to put a fresh spin on your workout. Here are some suggestions:

• **Explore the Variety Options and Gym Options.**

If you look at the Training Log pages in Chapter 10, you'll see that, along with the core routines, I've included two lists of extra exercises called "Gym Options" and "Variety Options." These may be swapped into the routine at your discretion to replace the prescribed exercises for the same body parts. Just follow the instructions at the beginning of the Training Log.

• **Shuffle the order.**

The sequence of body parts throughout the 12-week program is:

Chest
Back
Abs
Biceps
Triceps

Shoulders
Buttock and Hips
Legs
Stabilizers (Stabilizer exercises use several muscle groups to build functional strength and balance)

While sticking to the basic guideline of working from the center outward, you can vary the sequence of exercises by:

- Starting with upper body exercises one day and lower body the next.
- Swapping exercises for opposing muscle pairs: For example, instead of doing chest/back, do back/chest. Likewise, instead of biceps/triceps, do triceps/biceps.
- Working abs before *or* after other body parts.
- Following each exercise with a stretch aimed at the same muscle group. (Stretches are found in Chapter 9.)

- **Add more exercises for the same body part.**

Instead of just one exercise per body part, try doing two. Different exercises will tax the muscle differently, often leading to greater returns than you'd get by just doing more sets of the same exercise. Just be sure to balance opposing muscle groups. In other words, if you do two exercises for your biceps, do two for your triceps as well.

What Do I Do at the End of 12 Weeks?

My 12-week program is an example of what's called **periodization,** a formalized way of varying the stresses on your muscles by periodically changing the number of reps and the weight load. As you look at it more carefully, you'll see the program is divided into 3 blocks of 4 weeks each. Every 4 weeks, the exercises, rep goals, and (in some cases) the number of sets change to give your muscles a new challenge. The first block is aimed at gently easing your muscles into the program by using light weights and high reps. In the second block, the rep goals are lower to give you a chance to start using slightly heavier weights. By the third block, you're down in the rep range that enables you most efficiently to build strength, along with moderate contour.

Periodically changing your routine like this is the best way to keep it vital and challenging. At the end of the 12-week period, you have several choices:

• *Long-Range Option 1:*

Jump back to Block 1 and repeat the 12-week program. Since you'll be stronger this time around, you'll be using heavier weights and working at a higher intensity.

• *Long-Range Option 2:*

Stay in Block 3 for a while and continue to work on perfecting your form and improving your mental focus. Feel free to repeat Blocks 1 or 2 at any point. As you become stronger, increase your weights.

• *Long-Range Option 3:*

Maintain any of the blocks, designing your own changes to it, as described in the previous section:

- exchanging exercises with those from other blocks aimed at same body part
- varying the sequence
- adding in more exercises for same body part
- continuing to increase the weight whenever it gets too easy

> "I've been going to a gym now for 4 months and I couldn't be more pleased. I have definition in my arms, and my triceps muscle has quit jiggling. I love to show my friends my biceps!"
> Jan, age 48
> Laurel, MD

Important: You'll get the best results if you don't stay in the 10 to 12 rep range (Block 3) indefinitely, but occasionally cycle back through the higher rep ranges in Blocks 1 and 2.

At some point, you'll have gained enough self-confidence and knowledge of your body that you'll decide it's time to venture outside the bounds of this program. That's great! Explore new equipment at the gym, ask questions of knowledgeable friends or trainers, and experiment with new routines in the fitness magazines. Let what you've learned in your first few months of training help you decide what works for your body and what doesn't. By doing so, you'll develop an even greater sense of self-reliance and keep your routine interesting.

Stress, Overtraining, and Rest

An important part of long-term success is learning to gauge the stress your body is under at any given time, and find ways to keep it under control so it doesn't interfere with your progress.

You see, exercise itself is a form of stress—but a calculated one. We deliberately tax our muscles to encourage our body to become stronger. One of the benefits of doing this is that your body's adapting to the stresses of exercise creates a *cross-resistance* to other forms of stress as well. This is why staying in shape gives you an extra line of defense against infections or work pressure. Exercise is like a vaccine against life's pressures.

Stresses, however, can pile up to the point where your body is unable to adapt to them, and you become exhausted. If too many new challenges come at you at once, you may start feeling symptoms such as loss of appetite, disturbed sleep, or chronic fatigue. If unchecked, these can lead to more serious symptoms.

A GREAT FULL-BODY WORKOUT IN JUST TWO 20-MINUTE SESSIONS PER WEEK!

You don't need to train long if you're training *smart*. In creating the routines in this program, I've taken advantage of the latest research to create the fastest, most effective introduction to strength training possible. If you're new to weight training, you can get exceptional results with a very modest time investment. The important thing is to enter into it with intense mental focus and commitment. If you do that, I can promise you results you won't believe in just two fast-paced 20-minute sessions each week!

Here are some of the features of the *Lift Weights to Lose Weight* routines that make this possible:

1. **At first, just one set per body part.** Research shows that, as a newcomer, you can get 75 to 80 percent of the benefit of multiple sets by doing a single set of exercises for each body part.

2. **Minimal rest between sets and exercises.** Because a faster pace does a better job of overloading the muscles, a faster workout can also be a more effective one.

3. **Active rest between sets to save time.** You can use the rest time between sets or exercises to stretch the particular muscle you're working, saving you from having to stretch afterward.

4. **Just 2 workouts per week.** Studies show that 2 workouts a week will give you up to 80 percent of the gains you'd get from working out 3 or more times in a week.

5. **Modular routines to fit the smallest available workout windows.** Because the beneficial effects of strength training are cumulative, there's little or no difference between doing a 20-minute routine, or two 10-minute ones. My routines can be split into 10-minute modules, so you can squeeze in a few sets whenever you have the time.

If you're feeling any mild symptoms that seem to fit the profile of exhaustion, you could be training too hard, and if so, you should definitely cut back. However, the best approach is to look at *all* the sources of stress in your life—not just exercise—and ask yourself how many of them could be removed, at least temporarily. Exhaustion is the cumulative effect of all the sources of stress in our lives. Chances are, your exercise program is not your major source of stress.

Planned Breaks

It's a good idea to plan short layoffs at intervals in your training, as a proactive measure against overdoing it. I recommend taking a break of several days to a week every quarter or trimester throughout the year. It's okay to stay active during these periods—you can go for walks or enjoy other recreational activities—just give the weights a rest.

The routines in this program are designed to tax your body at a moderate level. Moderate exercise will help build your resistance to insulate you from the *real* stresses in your life.

In the past three chapters, we've laid a good foundation of basic strength training principles. As useful as I know this information to be, I realize the big hurdle for most people is the one that still looms ahead: taking action. Positive change will only begin when you put down this book, and pick up a weight. The last step in preparing for that moment is to address the practical questions of equipment and environment. Those will be covered in the next chapter.

Chapter 7

Home Is Where
the Gym Is

Now it's time to get down to the nuts and bolts of training. In this chapter, we'll discuss a range of issues having to do with equipment and setting, the basic *what* and *where* of working out. We'll discuss training at home versus training in a gym, and I'll explain how you can set up a good, basic home gym with the smallest possible investment of time and money.

Tools of the Trade

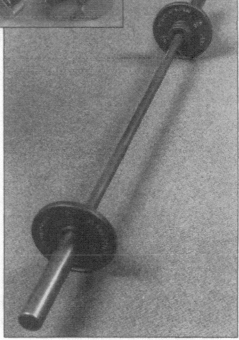

There are two basic classes of resistance devices:

Free Weights

Free weights, either **dumbbells** or **barbells**, are the standard handheld weights you picture when you think of weight lifting. Dumbbells are single-handed weights that can be used one at a time or in pairs. A barbell consists of a long metal bar, loaded at each end with iron plates of various sizes; lifting it requires both hands.

Weight Machines

Weight machines are mechanical devices that let you lift weights through a system of levers or cables.

People often ask me whether it's better to train with machines or free weights. The truth is, there are advantages to each. The first question to ask is whether you want to train at home or in the gym. If you're working out at home, most of your workout will be done using free weights, because they're more versatile and economical. If you're in a gym, you'll have both choices available and you can experiment to see which you prefer. Chances are you'll want to mix and match, to take advantage of the best that each system has to offer.

At Home, or in the Gym?

Gym training, or home training? You can get a good, basic workout in either place. It will be a little easier, however, to do your workout in a gym or health club because of the greater variety of equipment there. Still, equipment is just one factor to consider.

Through the years, I've gone back and forth about which environment I prefer. They address very different needs. Some days, I really want the range of choices available to me at the gym; at other times, the convenience and privacy of training at home outweighs all other considerations. The important thing is to work out—anyplace you'll actually *do* it is the right place!

Some of the issues affecting your decision might be:

• Social Support

Are you a people person? That camaraderie and support at a gym can make your workout a lot more fun. On the other hand, some people feel embarrassed about how they look when they're exercising, or are intimidated by all the fit bodies they see. Also, if you're more of a loner, you'd probably prefer a home setting.

> "The benefits of strength training are endless. I feel much stronger and have more confidence. My arms and legs are firm and toned. I don't have jiggling inner thighs anymore! I started with 5-pound dumbbells and now I'm using 12-pounders. My family is always telling me how good I look and how much younger I look."
> **Mayra, age 39**
> **Orlando, FL**

• Stimulation

The *energy* of a club, the noise and bustle, can be very stimulating. Loud music, television screens, a picture window through which you can watch a kickboxing class while you're cycling—all this may really get you moving, or it may make you want to dig a hole and hide! Consider your temperament.

• Structure

If you tend to need a kick in the pants to get yourself moving, you might benefit from the structure and peer pressure at the gym. If you're self-sufficient, you'll probably do well in either environment and can base your choice on other considerations.

Training in a Gym

Key benefit: Wide range of equipment options

A good gym or health club offers many benefits, including a wide range of equipment and facilities, access

ADVANTAGES OF GYM TRAINING
- social benefits: peer support, chance to make new friends
- high-energy environment
- more variety of equipment
- access to free or inexpensive aerobics classes
- access to other facilities such as a spa, sauna, track, or swimming pool

to friends and trainers, and a stimulating environment. For many people, the social aspects of a gym are as big a draw as the facilities themselves; both can potentially make working out more effective and more fun.

The only real hurdles to training at a gym are cost, and the challenge of disciplining yourself to get there on a regular basis. The cost to join will probably be more than you'd spend setting up a home gym, but, for many people, this is money well spent. And, depending on how your days are structured, going to a gym might actually be *more* convenient than training at home. If you work outside the home, for instance, visiting a nearby gym on your lunch hour can give you an energizing midday lift without taking any extra time at all!

ADVANTAGES OF HOME TRAINING

• no excuses

• no concerns about weather or road conditions

• no need to hire baby-sitters

• eliminates travel time: a 20-minute workout really can take just 20 minutes

• private: no one watching you sweat

• don't have to get dressed up

• always available

Training at Home

Key benefit: Convenience

Training at home is all about accessibility. If it's the middle of January, with a foot of snow on the ground, you can hole up there in your warm cocoon and get a great workout.

For someone just starting to train, a home gym might be the best way to go, and you can probably set one up for less than half the cost of a gym membership. It's true that you won't have access to some of the great equipment you'd have at a gym, but in the early stages this isn't critical. As a beginner, you can get great results simply using dumbbells and body weight. After a few months, you may decide to join a gym as well, and have the best of both worlds!

Selecting a Gym or Health Club

The best way to decide if working out in a gym is for you is to take a little field trip. If one of your friends belongs to a gym, ask to go along sometime. Most gyms will let you use their facilities for the day for a small fee—or even for free, if you tell them you're interested in joining. If you don't want any sales pitches, just go as a one-time guest of a friend. You might have to pay ten dollars or so, but they'll leave you alone and you can really scope out the place.

Walking into a gym for the first time, you may initially feel a bit overwhelmed. These days, the average health club looks like a vast factory, filled with acres of mysterious-looking contraptions. If it also happens to be throbbing with rock music, and teeming with 20-year-old hardbodies, you may be tempted to bolt for the exit.

Here are two comforting thoughts to bear in mind:

It's not as vast and impenetrable as it looks.

Your routine, at first, will only involve a tiny fraction of what's there. When you get ready to start the gym routine in this book, all you have to do is march up to the front desk with the routine in hand and say, "Show me where these particular weights and machines are." Once you get your bearings, you can refer to the exercise descriptions in this book to learn how to use the equipment.

You're not as conspicuous as you think.

Proper gym etiquette is to mind one's own business. You'll find that, for the most part, people will leave you alone while you work out, especially if you appear to want it that way. On the other hand, most people who train at a gym are enthusiastic about what they're doing and are happy to help you if you need assistance locating or adjusting a piece of gear. (One caution, though: Don't take anyone's training advice at face value unless you're sure they know their stuff!)

Making It Work at Home

Okay, so you've decided in favor of home training after all. Now what? In training at home, the main challenge you'll face is how to create and maintain *focus*. As much as home training offers the ultimate in convenience, it also offers the ultimate in distractions and interruptions. Phones, doorbells, kids, housework, and more all compete for your workout energy. In a gym, the environment focuses you on your task. At home, you have to provide the focus for yourself. Because there's no real physical separation between your workout area and your living area, you need to create a *psychological* separation.

Here are some guidelines for making it work at home:

• Dedicate a space.

Your workout will have more prominence in your life if it has more prominence in your home. After all, you have specific areas for cooking,

---

THINGS TO LOOK FOR IN A GYM

• Make sure your gym has a line of free weights in addition to machines.
Most of the exercises in our gym routines will involve free weights. You'll definitely need access to a set of dumbbells, and preferably barbells, too, although barbells are not essential to the 12-week program.

• Make sure you feel comfortable with the clientele and atmosphere.
Try to assess the general feel of the gym to decide whether you'll fit in. Different gyms attract different types of people. If you don't like the atmosphere at one gym, try another.

• Peak times—how crowded does it get?
Most gyms have rush hours when it may be difficult to get on your favorite equipment. Before joining, visit at the hours you're most likely to want to go, just to be sure the place isn't a zoo when you want to work out.

eating, sleeping, bathing, reading, and other activities—give your workout the same consideration. A couple of dumbbells stashed under the bed doesn't qualify as a home gym!

Now, this doesn't mean you have to set aside a whole room—a corner of a room or garage is enough. The point is to be consistent. If you train in the bedroom one day and on the back porch the next, it signals to your brain that it's not a very important activity. Dedicating space to it *makes* it important—and that place will give you a sense of power and purpose whenever you go there.

> "Because I have so many things needing my attention it's hard to exercise like I used to. But even when I don't have time for anything else, I can at least take time to lift weights. Although I still try to get out for walks with my children as often as possible for the aerobic benefits, I'm convinced weight training is what keeps me looking my best!"
> **Valerie**
> **Perkasie, PA**

• Block out the time.

The freedom to be spontaneous is one of the bonuses of training at home. Still, you can't leave your workout schedule too loose, or something else will always crowd in. Planning ahead is the best way to stay consistent. I like to sit down on Sunday to look over my schedule for the week and slot in my workout times. That doesn't mean I can't be flexible; it just means I know from the outset that I have time set aside for my workouts. I can shift them, but I'll have to rearrange other things.

Then, decide that when you're working out, you're unavailable for anything short of a true emergency. Don't pick up the phone, don't answer the door, and don't try to squeeze in unrelated tasks. After all, if you were at the gym, those things would have to wait. This will take some practice, but you can do it—remember, in the early stages, your workout's only 20 minutes long!

• Enlist the support of your family.

Your family can either be your biggest source of distractions or your biggest supporters—it all depends on how successfully you enlist their cooperation. Here's the secret: Don't just tell your kids you're working out. Go the extra step and tell them *why*. Sit them down and explain—in whatever words they're old enough to understand—why this is such an important time for you, *and for them*. Explain that your workout lifts your spirits, and makes you more patient and fun to be with. Do the same with your husband—be as direct and persuasive as you can. Make sure your whole family knows how vital this time is to your health and well-being.

But don't expect miracles! It took my kids a long time to understand that "Mommy's working out now" meant they shouldn't come ask me for a glass of juice. Over time, they did understand and respect it.

• **Recruit a friend.**

A great way to raise the energy level at home is to bring in a workout partner. Maybe there's someone right in your neighborhood who could join you for workouts—and maybe share the cost of the equipment as well. Training with a partner can be a huge morale-booster.

Home Gym Equipment

In setting up a home gym, the limitations are always space and money. I've mentioned the value of a dedicated space; it needn't be large, though. All you need is enough room to stand, sit, and lie down, preferably without having to move things around between exercises. As far as equipment goes, it doesn't take much at first. Here's a list of the basics:

Dumbbells

If you're starting to train for the first time or feel that you are very out of shape, I recommend purchasing the following assortment of dumbbells:

3, 5, 8, 10 pounds

As you become stronger, you'll also need 12-, 15-, and 20-pound dumbbells to be able to properly overload the muscles. If you have trained before or feel you have a good basic level of strength, you can skip the 3-pound weights and get:

5, 8, 10, 12, 15, 20 pounds

> "A few years ago, I asked my husband to get me a set of 5- and 8-pound weights. Men always seem to think that bigger is better—he bought me sets of 10, 15, 20, and 25-pound weights. Well, I used them! The next day, my arms were so rubbery I couldn't even reach up to rub my nose! But I didn't give up, and now I use them every day. I feel stronger, have more energy, and even though my weight hasn't changed much, my clothes sure do fit better!"
> **Karen, age 43**
> **Charlotte, NC**

In the early stages, at least, you should be able to get a great workout with weights of 20 pounds or less, although you may eventually develop enough strength to require more. For reference, the dumbbell set I use at home goes up to 50 pounds, but I rarely lift more than 25 pounds. For most women, an upper range of 15 to 25 pounds is ample.

I prefer fixed-weight dumbbells to adjustable models because they save a tremendous amount of time. However, another option is the ProBell system. With the ProBell, you dial in the resistance you want while the dumbbell is still sitting on the rack, and it automatically picks up the right number of plates when you lift it. One ProBell takes up the same space as a single set of dumbbells, but gives you six sets in one.

Floor Mat

If your workout area isn't carpeted, you'll need a mat of some kind for sit-ups and stretching.

Bench (Optional) or Chair

A training bench is one of the most useful pieces of gear you can own. Available in sporting goods stores and catalogues, training benches are padded and some can be adjusted from level to inclined positions. If you're not quite ready to make the investment, most exercises that use a bench can also be done either with a chair or on the floor.

Personal Accessories

I recommend keeping a towel and some drinking water handy. And, if listening to energetic music helps you focus, by all means set up a radio or stereo nearby.

Adding to Your Home Gym

I don't usually recommend investing in machines for home use. Weight machines are expensive and fairly specialized, meaning that there are only a few exercises you can do on each machine. Nor do I recommend the majority of the "20-exercises-in-one" gadgets that promise a total-body workout with one piece of equipment—they're usually only good for training one or two body parts, and awkward or ineffective for the rest. As a result, they're notorious for getting used once and then stashed under the stairs. If you're going the home training route, it makes the most sense to start with a basic dumbbell set and add pieces over time. Possible additions could include:

Barbells

Useful for Bench Press and Squats.

Exercise Balls

The inflatable exercise ball, or stability ball, was developed by physical therapists in Switzerland, and is a versatile and fun-to-use home fitness device. By lying, bouncing, or rocking on the ball in various ways, you can achieve extremely effective stretching, warm-up, and muscle toning. The regular-size ball is 55 centimeters in diameter, and is recommended for persons under 5 foot 10. A 65-centimeter ball is also available from most suppliers.

Cardio Equipment

For my money, the most useful type of home cardio equipment is a treadmill. If you decide to invest in a treadmill, be sure you get one that can operate on an incline so as to increase the intensity. Also popular are elliptical machines (in which you perform a walking motion while your feet remain in contact with the floating "pedals"); they're easy on the knees and provide a fun change of pace.

Which Are Better— Free Weights or Weight Machines?

Hard-core gym-goers love to debate this question. Once again, it comes down to personal preference and goals. Weight machines are convenient and easy to use, while getting the best results with free weights requires more knowledge and attention to detail. However, free weights provide greater versatility and functional benefits. Here, in brief, are how the two systems stack up.

Free Weights

• More similar to real-world tasks

When using free weights, your body has to balance and stabilize itself, just as it would in everyday situations. This develops your coordination and creates a more functional kind of strength—one that's more useful in daily life.

• Freedom of movement

Instead of being locked into a certain posture by the framework of a machine, free weights allow you to adjust yourself to find the position that best suits your body.

• Versatility

Unlike machines, one set of weights can be used for dozens of exercises, allowing for plenty of variety in your routine.

Weight Machines

• Simplicity

Machines are easy to learn, and easy to use.

• Safety

Machines have a safety margin over free weights because if your strength gives out, most machines are designed to prevent the weight from falling on you. Machines are not without risk, though; it's easy to pinch fingers or pull muscles if you're not careful.

Although free weights are more versatile, machines can provide good basic conditioning, and they're great for adding variety. And certain exercises are easier to do with machines, which is why the best workout uses a combination of both.

• Variety

Although it's possible to get a full-body workout on my program using nothing but dumbbells and body weight, the great thing about gym training is variety. Switching exercises will not only keep your interest up, it will stimulate the muscles in new and different ways, and can actually improve your results. In the routines that follow, you'll find machine-oriented options for many of the free weights exercises.

• Configuration of machine encourages proper form

The fact that proper body alignment is built in to the machine helps the beginner get results right away, with minimal instruction. On the other hand, to the extent that a machine helps to stabilize your body, your muscles don't get the same balancing and stabilizing challenge they might with free weights. Also, machines are only adjustable within certain limits; if you're particularly short or tall, you may have a hard time using some of the less-adjustable models.

My Favorite Machines

When you first look around the gym, the machines may all look alike. But, in fact, there are a few standouts—machines that work the muscles in ways that would be difficult, if not impossible, using free weights.

Some of my favorites are:

Lat Pull-down machine, and others involving cables and pulleys, are actually close relatives of free weights. Like free weights, they afford freedom of movement and encourage coordination among stabilizing muscles. The strength you gain will translate well to everyday situations.

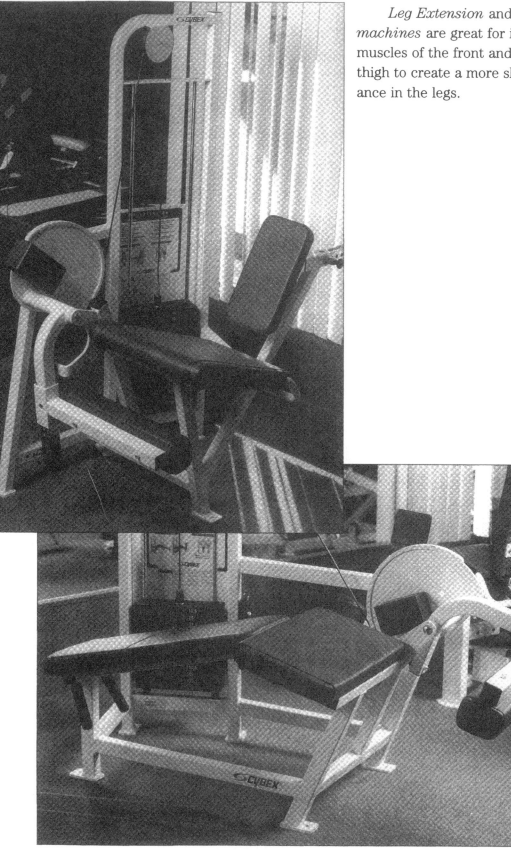

Leg Extension and *Leg Curl machines* are great for isolating the muscles of the front and back of the thigh to create a more shapely appearance in the legs.

The *Leg Press machine* is a relative of lunges and squats, and develops leg strength that will come in handy in dozens of daily tasks.

Where's the best place to train? *Anywhere you put your mind to it!* Whether it's the hottest new health club in town, or the little corner at home next to the water heater, it really doesn't matter. What matters is that you've made the commitment to train. With the help of a few well-chosen pieces of gear, you'll be able to use the routines in this book to get fantastic results—anywhere!

Chapter 8

Making It Happen

I have a favorite icebreaker I use when speaking to groups at book sign-ings or seminars. I say, "Okay, you've got the information...let's get to the bottom line: *What's your excuse?*" And I listen while the audience mem-bers give me their best reasons why they *can't,* or *won't,* work out. To start the ball rolling, I tell them, "Anybody who's got an excuse I haven't heard before gets a free video."

I always enjoy hearing the excuses. Although some are quite origi-nal ("My hair gets kinky when I sweat"), they all fall into a few basic cat-egories:

> *I don't have time.*
> *I just don't enjoy it.*
> *(Many variations on this: I get hot, I get bored, etc.)*
> *I'm not sure what to do or how to do it.*
> *I have physical limitations that prevent me.*

Time management, boredom, discomfort, physical limitations—all these problems have solutions, if we're open to them. I'll cover some of them in this chapter. More important, though, is the underlying issue of whether you're really open to a solution at all.

Problem Solvers and Problem Makers

There are very few, if any, external obstacles to success. It's true! For every problem you can name, I can point to someone who overcame it. As long as you're still breathing, there are no insurmountable obstacles.

Now, that's not to say there aren't occasional hurdles. If you're holding down two jobs, or you're a single mom with six kids, or if you've just thrown your back out, you may have some difficulty getting to the gym. But the fact is, most problems can be overcome if you've got the desire. Think about the last time you really wanted something. Desire finds a way.

Of course, you have to be realistic. Some hurdles you can jump, but others you may have to detour around. The point is to stay focused on whatever will bring you *closer* to your goal. This is what it means to be a creative problem solver.

When I broke my leg a few years ago, everyone told me I wouldn't be able to do aerobic exercise. I didn't buy it. Instead, I asked around and found a gym that had an upper body ergometer—a bicycle-like machine that you pedal with your hands. I tried it and was dripping with sweat in no time. Later on, since my cast allowed me to bend at the knee, I found I could get on a stationary bicycle and pedal it with one leg. And, since I could still do all my upper body weight lifting exercises, I hardly had to make any concession at all to that broken leg.

Over the years, I've tried to make it a habit to be a problem solver. When I'm hit with a challenge, I start making phone calls: I explore, I ask questions. For me, taking action has become a natural response.

On the other hand, there's another type of person, one that seems to constitute about 20 percent of any group I talk to. This person is a fountain of excuses, and will shoot holes in all your suggestions. These people are creative problem *makers*. Problem makers won't let you solve their problem because, actually, they're not looking for a solution. They're looking for an excuse to stay put.

If you find you always have a reason why *now* is not a good time to do something beneficial for your health, you may be using minor problems as an excuse for your unwillingness to take action. But what's behind this immobility? How do you step out of your problem-maker mind-set?

I'm convinced that at least part of the problem maker's self-inflicted paralysis has to do with having no clear idea where they want to go. Their goal isn't real to them; they haven't *inspired* themselves to action. So let's look now at an 8-step plan to wake yourself up, get yourself moving—and make it happen!

STEP 1: SET YOUR PRIORITIES

Usually when you ask people to list the things that are important to them, health will be in the top three. They may list their family, God, making a contribution to the planet…these others vary between people, but the wish to remain healthy is universal. If that really is the case—if you really believe your health has an effect on the quality of your life—then you'd put things that improved your health and well-being high on your to-do list, right? The funny thing is, most of us don't live that way.

The first step in organizing your life is to define your priorities. Decide what it is you really want most. If you can distill your goals down to a simple statement of purpose, it will give you a beacon to follow through the hectic and distracting crush of daily life.

For example, I have a mission statement for my life that goes like this: *To improve the lives of people around the world by creating quality health and fitness products to educate, motivate, and inspire.* As you can see, this statement doesn't spell out what I'm going to be doing on any given day. It simply gives me a star to steer by, a way to make sure I'm on course.

STEP 2: INSPIRE YOURSELF

Motivation doesn't just happen by itself. If it did, there'd be no need for halftime pep talks, patriotic songs, or million-dollar soft drink ads. Motivation comes from the emotional implications of facts. If you think of a time when you felt a seemingly effortless surge of motivation to do something, it's probably because some piece of information set off a train of thought in you that caused you to have an emotional response. You heard your favorite store was having a sale and you suddenly visualized that new dress you wanted, and imagined how great you'd *feel* when you wore it. So you dashed out on your lunch hour and bought it.

Motivation occurs when something engages your emotions. It begins when you're presented with an image of what you want, and a way to get it. The more vividly the image is presented and the more it seems to be associated with positive feelings, the more it will begin to inspire you emotionally to want it, and the easier it will be to get moving in the direction of getting it. This is the magic that advertisers attempt to work on us every day.

You can follow this strategy to motivate yourself. In the previous pages, you've read about the benefits, and the basic techniques, of weight training. Now it's time to get your imagination working—and, most important, to engage your emotions as well. To get started, try a little visualization:

• Really focus on the benefits of weight lifting as described in Chapter 2 and try to imagine in detail what it would be like to have them yourself. First, think about people you know who never exercise. Think about women you know in your mother's generation who've suffered from loss of muscle and bone density. Look at women ten years older than yourself. Look at their weight, their skin tone; think about their ailments and complaints. Try and imagine what you might look and feel like in ten years if—God forbid!—you don't exercise. Try and construct detailed pictures in your head of all these scenarios. Make them as real as you can. Then, think about people you know who do exercise regularly. Think about how much better they look since they started exercising. Imagine how you'll look when you do the same.

• Now imagine yourself doing the routine in this book. Walk through the whole 12 weeks in your mind. Imagine yourself feeling awkward at first, but becoming much more assured and stronger in just a few weeks. Visualize yourself at the end of 12 weeks with twice the strength you have now: standing taller, feeling more powerful and self-assured. Imagine yourself in some specific situation a few months from now when it would really make a difference to you to be looking and feeling stronger, more fit, and more confident.

The many benefits of strength training should be motivating in themselves. But there's nothing more human than knowing what's best and still not doing it. Visualizing the benefits, painting the picture vividly in your mind, and then *putting yourself in the picture* will help stimulate desire. These mental techniques can bring you to the brink of action. Then, it's time to jump.

STEP 3: A 12-WEEK PROMISE TO YOURSELF

There are things in life you don't know you feel strongly about until you actually experience them. Being in shape is like that: the great, indescribable feeling of energy, the vitality and power, the spring you'll feel in your muscles and movements all day long...I believe if I can get you to feel this way, your motivation to continue will take care of itself. The first step, though, is an act of faith.

So here's the deal: I want you to make a very easy, short-term commitment. I'm not asking you to commit to a lifelong change, or even a very big change. Lasting change is accomplished one step at a time. I'm simply asking you to conduct a 12-week experiment with your body, to find out just how great you can feel. Put my program to the test. Follow it with full diligence and focus—for just 12 weeks.

Put It in Writing

I urge you to document your commitment. To help you do this, I've provided a form that I call my 12-Week Promise. It is a contract between you and *yourself,* a pledge to take on and complete the 12-week program in this book. Read it over and think about it. By signing it, you will be making a solemn promise to yourself to follow through.

Once you've signed the form, display it in your home in a place where you'll see it frequently. If possible, put it somewhere your friends and family will see it, too. If you're working out at home, hang it on the wall in the area you've designated as your home gym.

Let Me Help!

If you want to really motivate yourself, send a copy of your commitment form to me, here at Kathy Smith Lifestyles, and I'll hold it on file in my office. That way, I'll know that you've made the decision to follow the program, and *you'll* know that I'm counting on you to honor your promise! At the end of the twelve weeks, send in the Completion Stub on the bottom of the form to let me know that you did it. When I receive that stub, I'll publish your name on the Kathy Smith *Lift Weights to Lose Weight* Honor Roll on my Web site at www.KathySmith.com. The Honor Roll will list the names of everyone who follows and completes my program, so that all the visitors to my Web site can celebrate your achievement.

You'll find the 12-Week Promise form in Appendix A at the end of the book.

STEP 4: KEEP IT MANAGEABLE

For some people, the hard part is just getting started. Other people, though, are great starters, and dive into every new thing that comes along. Their challenge is to stay focused and motivated over time. For some of us it's easy to start strong, but then become disorganized, erratic, overambitious, perfectionistic—these are all ways we sabotage our prospects. Some tips for keeping your program under control once you've started:

Use Your Training Log

The Training Log in this book is designed to make this program as easy and manageable as possible. The log does two things. First, it shows you exactly what to do in every workout, with pictures of all the exercises to help you along. Second, it gives you a record of your progress.

Use the log to create a workout schedule and hold yourself to it. Start on each Sunday. Look at your week and block out your workout times for that week. Remember that there are various ways you can schedule the workouts—you can do your whole body on one day, or break it up into segments (such as upper and lower body) and do the two halves on alternate days. Once you've got your week scheduled, treat working out with the same sense of responsibility as you would paying bills or packing the kids' lunches.

Start Gradually

People sometimes feel they have to fix everything in their life at once. Thinking that way can be paralyzing. Instead, just do *something*. Just start. If you can only do 6 of the 10 exercises, that's fine. Or maybe you have to start even smaller. If the thought of *any* sort of training routine is just too big a bite to swallow, try this: Take a short, brisk walk around the neighborhood. Walking for even 10 minutes is guaranteed to improve your outlook and increase your determination to do more. Do this every day until you're ready to progress further. There's no such thing as too small a step—if it's in the right direction.

> "I drew up a calendar to take me through February. I gave myself a stamp for each completed workout, although I could change days around if I felt like it. By summer, I had really changed the way I looked. My face looked sharper and brighter and my arms had really toned up. I'm still at it. I try not to focus on the end result or perfection, but on looking healthy and feeling good about myself and my effort. Lifting weights has really made me feel strong mentally, emotionally, and physically."
>
> Jill, age 34
> Seattle, WA

Be Consistent

Interviewers often ask me to name the most important thing about working out. That's easy: consistency! The most powerful forces in our lives are our *habits*. You probably have a number of things in your life (for better or worse) that you do habitually, without thinking. If you can make exercise one of them, you've won the battle. I have a hard time even telling people what my exercise "regimen" is because I don't think of it that way. Being physically active is woven into the fabric of my life; I don't think of it as a separate thread.

Be Flexible

Fitness doesn't have to be an all-or-nothing goal. My days are crazy sometimes. I'll be doing, say, a morning show in New York, staying in a hotel. It would be easy to let my routine slide. Instead, I run downstairs to the hotel's workout room, do a five-minute warm-up and 10 or 15 minutes of weights. Even that little dose is enough to keep my muscles stimulated and keep me feeling on track. The point is, if you wait for conditions to be perfect, you will never do anything.

So be creative—have alternate plans. What happens when you travel? Find out in advance where the exercise facilities are. What if it's snowing, or you can't find a baby-sitter, so you can't get to your health club? Have a place you can work out at home. Nothing is more predictable than life's unpredictability—so *plan* to improvise!

STEP 5: FIND REWARDS ALONG THE WAY

Although some people are very disciplined and can make themselves do something purely for the sake of long-range goals, we're not all like that. To stick with a program, most of us need reinforcement along the way— the more, the better! We may brush our teeth every day because we know the long-term importance of oral hygiene. Still, there's an immediate pay-off: clean teeth look and feel better. Whenever you can find in-the-moment reasons for doing something, it makes it that much easier.

Physical Sensation

When I think of weight training, I think of how it makes me *feel*. I wish I could snap my fingers and implant this sensation in your head for five minutes. More than anything else, I think it's the pure, physical sensation it produces in my body that keeps me motivated.

It wasn't always this way, though. Frankly the sensation of physical effort itself—what you feel *during* your workout—takes a little getting used to. I honestly didn't like it at first. The solution is to find positive ways to think about it. Here's a little mental exercise you can try:

Let's say it's your first week of the program. You start to work out. Within a few moments, you begin to feel a variety of new sensations in your body that you may at first label as discomfort. "I'm breathing hard, I'm hot, I'm tired, this doesn't feel good! I want to stop! My body's telling me to stop!"

Take a moment, right then, to analyze exactly what you're feeling. Really try to get inside the feeling and experience it without labeling it. Ask yourself:

Is my heart racing?

Stop for a moment and breathe slowly. Visualize your blood rushing oxygen to your muscles.

Do I feel hot?

Notice how the air is moving against your skin, evaporating the perspiration and cooling your skin. Think of your body as a beautiful machine, all systems working smoothly as they were designed to.

Try another set. Then stop and assess. Is there really anything *intolerable* about what you're feeling? Probably not. Just unfamiliar sensations. Begin to find positive ways to think about these sensations. Instead of discomfort, think of it as heat, excitement, arousal, alertness, strength, power.

Over time, these unfamiliar sensations will be a big part of what keeps you coming back for more. Results are important—but results are long-term. Long-term results and in-the-moment sensations work together to keep you motivated.

THE PAYOFF

Find the payoff at every stage. Don't just focus on the long-range goal; have mid-range and short-range reasons for what you're doing.

In School:

Long-term goal:	a diploma and good job
Mid-range benefit:	learning things that interest me
Day-to-day benefit:	an entertaining teacher; seeing friends

In Your Workout:

Long-term goal:	longer life; better long-term quality of life; my ideal figure
Mid-range benefit:	beginning to look and feel fit
Day-to-day benefit:	physical sensations of working out; exercise high; fun with workout partner; stress relief; social outlet

---

"If I don't feel like working out, I make a deal with myself: Just do upper body. . . . I always end up doing the whole [workout]! I always feel good about myself when I am done, too!"
Tiffany, age 32
Pittsburgh, PA

STEP 6: CUT BITE-SIZE PIECES

Most of us do want to improve our bodies and feel better. The problem is, we're just not in touch with the emotional drive to exercise on a daily basis. There are plenty of days when, despite your good intentions, you just want to switch off the alarm and go back to sleep. The solution here is the same one you'd use to get your four-year-old to eat her peas. Stop thinking about your workout as a whole, and just concentrate on one bite at a time.

The "baby steps" technique.

On a day when you don't feel like working out, make a deal with yourself to simply get dressed in your workout clothes. Your brain will take this as a signal that the decision to work out has been made. You'll be surprised how well this works. By *acting as if* you were going to work out, you can get your body to perform, even if you don't feel like it. I don't know how many times the simple act of putting on my running shoes has been enough to get me moving and out the door.

The "one more exercise" game.

Tell yourself, "I'll just do one more set." Then, as you're doing that one set, tell yourself again, "Just one more." Decide that you're allowed to stop anytime you want, but just keep cajoling yourself into one more exercise. Amazingly, this works even though you *know* you're pulling your strings. Why? Because, deep down, you also know you're doing a good thing. Before you know it, you're done!

STEP 7: WORK OUT WITH A PARTNER

Probably the single biggest secret to a great workout is to train with a partner. Having a training partner is a way to harness some of the group energy you feel in an aerobics class, and bring it to your strength training. Even though I'm usually able to discipline myself to train alone, I know I get a much better workout with a partner. Here are some of the benefits of training with a friend:

Keep each other consistent and accountable.

There are bound to be days when you'd just as soon forget you ever heard of weight training. Having a partner increases the chances that at least one of you will be fired up and ready to go. One day your partner provides the motivating energy; the next day it's your turn. We all know it's easier to urge someone else to do what's good for them than to do it ourselves. With a partner, you can provide this service for each other!

Spot each other for safety.

Spotting someone means standing by to help them during any exercise where they might be injured if they lost control of the weights. Although the exercises in my basic routines can all be done safely without a spotter, having a spotter becomes important if you decide to experiment with exercises such as Straight Bar Bench Press.

Boost intensity by providing an assist.

Assisted reps, also known as *forced reps,* is a technique in which your partner provides just a little help to get you through extra reps you wouldn't have been able to do on your own. Forcing reps is an advanced technique and I don't recommend it during the first 12 weeks. It's very effective for increasing workout intensity, but, as a result, it can leave you quite sore the next day.

Provide a psychological incentive.

Your training partner can help push you in a variety of ways, both by cheering you on, and by providing a little healthy competition. Many people find that simply having an audience causes them to work with greater intensity.

Make your workout more fun.

Having someone to talk and joke with makes the time fly by. If you're training at a gym, you can carpool, and even incorporate your workout into a shopping trip or other excursion.

STEP 8: LEARN TO MANAGE YOUR TIME

By far, one of the most popular excuses for not working out is lack of time. It goes without saying that we all have hectic lives. As a businesswoman and mother, I think I'm as busy as anyone! But when you get to a point that you can't find 15 or 20 minutes each day for yourself, you've got to stop and examine your life.

When you say you're too busy to exercise, what are you really saying? You don't have time for something that will give you *more* energy? Something that will stimulate your creative juices and increase your enjoyment of life? This is like insisting on working in the dark because you don't have time to stop and turn on a light.

Stresses are a natural consequence of living in the world. The trick is to stay in control of it all, to make choices based on your own sense of what's important. Here are some tips to help you manage your time:

> "When [my niece and I] decided we needed to start working out, we decided we should work together for moral support. Not only [has training] strengthened our muscles, but it's also strengthened our relationship."
> Rory and Cindy
> Massillon, OH

Examine how you spend your time.

Are all the things you do really helping you toward your goals? How much TV do you watch? How much time do you spend talking on the phone? How much of your day is dictated by other people's agendas? Do you really not have enough time, or are you just not spending it in the right places?

Learn to discriminate.

Learn to make judgments about what's important and what's not. If my friend is having a real crisis, I can make a quick decision that my workout can wait until evening. At the same time, I'll make a mental note about whatever else needs to be moved to accommodate the change of plans. Perhaps I'll skip my run to the dry cleaners or forgo a bit of late-night catalogue browsing.

Learn to consolidate.

Imagine what life would be like if you went to the market before preparing every single meal—you'd spend half your day shopping for food! That's why most of us consolidate our marketing, at least for staple foods. Find ways to group together your other errands and chores, and you'll save a tremendous amount of time. Instead of answering the phone every time it rings, for instance, I let the machine take messages and return all the calls in one sitting at the end of the day.

Learn to say no.

This is tough for many of us. Often, though, an alternative is to take requests others make of you and creatively reframe them to fit *your* priorities. If a friend asks, "Can you take me to the airport?" you might say, "Actually, it's a busy day for me. Why don't you let me be your backup if you can't get someone else to take you?" Saying it this way, you're not abandoning your friend: You're there for her if she's really in need, but otherwise you're making it clear you've got your own schedule to keep.

Don't hide behind "emergencies."

There are plenty of urgent demands on our time. Phone calls, bills to pay, household chores—you can easily fill your day with these matters. The problem is, living this way doesn't get you anywhere; it's just treading water. It's not that you can, or should, ignore the pressing day-to-day matters. The point is to always be on the lookout for truly important things, things that will actually make your life better. If your whole day goes by without your doing at least one thing, however small, aimed at bettering your life, then something's wrong.

So, let me ask you the same question I ask the audience at my seminars: "What's your excuse?" No excuse? All right, then. Let's get started!

Chapter 9

Warm Up and Stretch

I've been practicing yoga for many years now and I love it. I'm particularly intrigued by the Eastern idea of energy flow—of moving *chi,* or energy, through your body. The more freely the energy flows, the healthier and more energetic you feel. When energy is blocked, areas of the body may become tight; over time they can become rigid, even painful. In yoga, as in tai chi, the goal is to keep the body supple through movement and stretching.

Whenever I spend an hour in a yoga class, I enter a kind of meditative state and emerge feeling tremendously relaxed and refreshed. But you know what? You don't have to study yoga to get the benefits of increased flexibility. As much as I love it, I can't always find the time to squeeze an hour-long class into my schedule. A better way is to learn a few simple stretches and incorporate them into your daily routine.

A simple flexibility routine will provide a wide range of benefits. In this chapter, you'll learn ten easy stretches that will allow you to stretch out your whole body in just a few minutes.

You'll get the *best* results if you go a step further, and make the release of tension a habit throughout your day. I do this unconsciously. Sometimes, when I'm talking on the phone, I'll have one leg up on the counter, stretching out my hamstrings. Wherever I am—in a meeting, on a

> *"I have always been an exercise enthusiast and considered myself in excellent shape, but after the birth of my second child, I began to have lower back and neck pain. Since I've been working out with weights, my back and neck pain is nonexistent."*
>
> Barbara, age 43
> San Diego, CA

plane—I try to find ways to work out those little areas of tightness. My mantra is *decompression*—take the pressure off, elongate, and create a sense of space throughout the body.

The Benefits of Stretching

For most of us, our daily activities do not promote suppleness and freedom of motion. When we sit all day at work, our muscles tighten; in time our body starts to feel locked and compressed. Age, too, makes us stiffer. You may notice it when tying your shoes, or turning to look over your shoulder in the car. And yet, with just a few minutes of effort a day, it's possible to actually become *more* flexible as we get older. This is one of the most overlooked areas of fitness, and the benefits are enormous.

• Improve Your Posture

Excessively tight muscles can actually hold your body in a hunched or poorly aligned posture. Stretching and loosening up the muscles of the back, shoulders, and hips will make it much easier to stand tall and straight.

• Move with Greater Ease

There's a reason dancers spend so much time stretching. Good flexibility is essential for creating fluid, unrestricted movement. Regular stretching will promote an easy grace that will make all activities more enjoyable.

• Protect Yourself from Injury in Daily Activity

If you've ever been on skis or Rollerblades, you know how easy it is to suddenly find that one leg is going east while the other's going west. Sudden stretching forces like this aren't limited to sports, though; they occur in many daily activities. The ability to absorb an unexpected stretching force without getting hurt is all a matter of flexibility.

• Protect Yourself from the Stresses of Weight Training

Working your muscles with weights can sometimes create muscle tension. I find that stretching after, or even *during*, my weight routine is a great way to keep the muscles relaxed and keep my energy flowing.

• Promote Spinal Health and Prevent Lower Back Problems

Because we sit so much, the muscles that flex and extend our legs may become shortened. This affects the way you move when bending and lifting, and may place awkward (asymmetrical) stresses on your lower back. Stretching the hip muscles will help keep your back safe and pain-free.

• Relax and Recharge

There's something about the slow, deliberate pace of stretching and the deep breathing involved that just seems to melt the stress from your body. It releases both physical and mental tension. In fact, a few minutes of light stretching before going to bed is one of the best "sleeping pills" I know.

Warming Up

The first stage of your workout should be a warm-up. Although gentle stretching can be a part of your warm-up, the best warm-up involves controlled, full-range movement using the muscles you're planning to train. The purpose is to raise the temperature of the muscles and increase circulation. Five minutes of any light activity that involves those muscles will work. Walking or light jogging are good ways to warm up the legs; light dumbbells, calisthenics, or rowing are good warm-ups for the arms. Again, the warm-up is for limbering. You're not trying to increase your flexibility or tax your muscles— you're simply "oiling the machine" before your workout.

Here are some specific suggestions for warming up:

> "I feel strong and I see the changes in my body. My arms have shape, my legs are much stronger, and my abs are flat! I am more energetic and confident. It has also helped my posture. Now I like to wear sleeveless shirts and short skirts to show off my legs. Before lifting weights I was a size 10; now I'm a size 7."
> Glorymar, age 24
> San Juan, PR

• Flowing, rhythmic movement to stimulate circulation: Swing or circle your arms; do leg swings, kicks, or knee lifts. If you like, you can intersperse these with gentle stretching of about 10 seconds per stretch, aimed at working out the stiffness, without pushing beyond your normal range.

• Choose a very light dumbbell (1-, 3-, or 5-pound) and do a set of exercises for the muscles you're going to be working. Use enough weight so that you feel *some* resistance to the movement, but not enough to fatigue the muscle or put any strain on the joint. A typical upper body warm-up might consist of 8 to 12 reps each of:

Standing Biceps Curl
One-Arm Triceps Press
Lateral Raise
Overhead Press
Rear Raise

• Several minutes of cycling, easy jogging, rowing, or running in place.

Ten Easy Stretches

Stretching is one of the simplest, most beneficial forms of conditioning. The stretching routine that follows will take you no more than 5 to 10 minutes, and is guaranteed to build greater flexibility and poise, reduce your risk of injury, and relax and rejuvenate your whole body. Because the time investment is so small and the rewards so great, I recommend doing this routine every day if possible, or at least three times a week. On days when you lift weights, use the stretching routine as a cool-down afterward.

"Now that I'm 43 years old, I realize that it is so important to keep my bones strong, and weight lifting is important to me for that reason. My muscle mass is probably close to what it was in my twenties. I'm sure that's one reason people think I'm younger than I really am. Having more muscle means that my metabolism is running higher as well. Any extra weight I gain slips off in no time."

Karen
Charlotte, NC

Active Recovery

If you don't want to take the time to do the entire stretching routine at the end of your weight workout, you can sneak the stretches into the weight routine itself, during your recovery periods between sets and exercises. When you've finished working a particular muscle, perform the stretch for that muscle. This technique is called *active recovery,* and can be a real time-saver if you're in a hurry.

Stretching Guidelines

Warm up for 3 to 5 minutes before stretching using gentle, fluid, rhythmic movement. Always stretch in a slow, controlled manner. You should feel a sensation of tension, but not actual pain. Use your breathing to help you relax into each position, gradually increasing your range without bouncing or bobbing. Hold each stretch for 10 to 30 seconds.

Do not stretch if you feel any sharp pains in your joints or muscles, or if osteoporosis is suspected. Consult with your doctor if you feel pain or have any questions about whether a stretching program is appropriate for you.

1. Hamstring/Calf Stretch

Sit on the edge of a chair and extend your right leg straight in front of you, keeping the left knee bent and left foot flat on the floor. Lean forward at the hip, keeping your back straight. Rest your hands on your thighs to control the stretch. Feel the stretch along the back of your right leg. At the same time, pull the foot of the extended leg up toward you, feeling the stretch in the back of your calf. Switch legs and repeat.

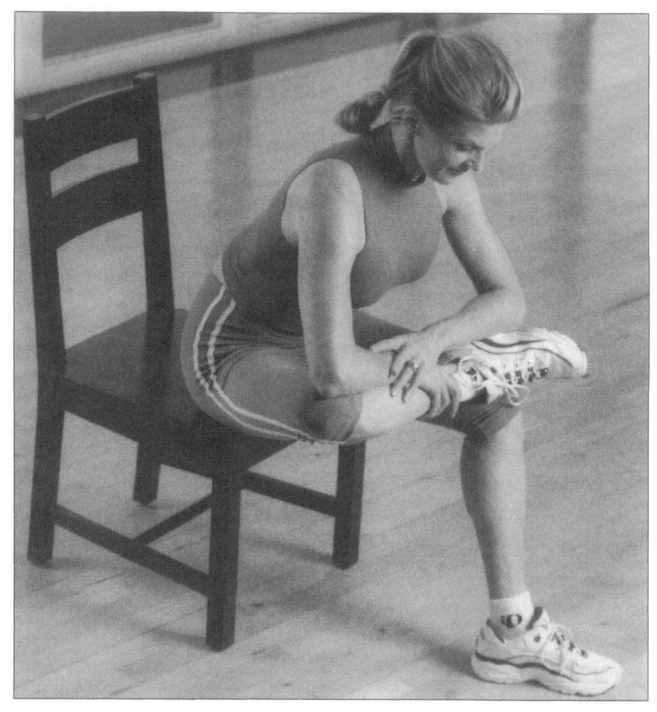

2. Hips/Buttocks/Lower Back Stretch

From a seated position, rest the ankle of one leg on the knee of the other.
Lean forward, keeping your back straight, feeling for a stretch in the side
of your hip. Switch legs and repeat.

3. Rotary Torso Stretch

Sit with your knees and hips at right angles and your feet flat on the floor. With your left hand resting on the outside of your right knee and your right forearm on the back of the chair, twist your torso to the right. Use your arms for leverage to help you twist, and look back over your shoulder as you do so. Keep your upper back straight. Feel the stretch along the sides of your waist and chest. Switch sides and repeat.

4. Front of Hip/Chest/Front of Shoulder Stretch

Sit sideways on the edge of a chair with your inside leg bent at the knee, and your foot flat on the floor as in a normal seated position. Extend the outside leg behind you, with knee slightly bent. Your legs should be in the position of a deep lunge. Feel the stretch in the front of your upper thigh and hip.

At the same time, clasp your hands behind your back. Straighten your arms, then lift your hands and chest. Take a deep breath and feel your chest expanding. You'll feel a stretch in the front of your shoulders, too. Switch legs and repeat.

5. Rear Shoulder/Neck Stretch

Sit with your knees together, feet flat on the floor, and raise your right arm
in front of you to shoulder height, or a little less. Grasp your right arm with
your left hand, and pull your right arm across your body. At the same time,
drop your head to your left shoulder. You'll feel the stretch along the right
side of your neck, as well as in your right shoulder and upper arm. Repeat
with your left arm.

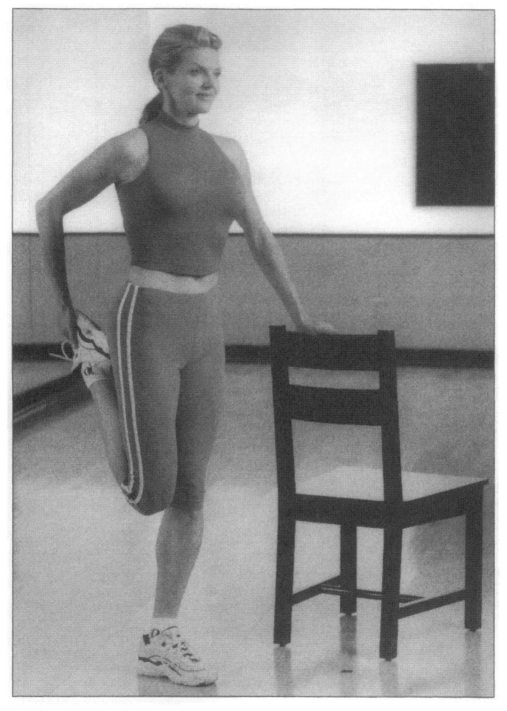

6. Quad/Hip Flexor Stretch

Using your left hand to steady yourself on a chair, grasp your right foot behind you with your right hand. Pull your heel gently toward your buttocks. Slightly contract your abdominals to avoid arching your back. Keep your knees together and hips facing forward. Switch legs and repeat.

Pay attention to your alignment. Make sure your body stays tall without twisting, and the knee of the stretched leg points straight down.

7. Outer Hip/Torso Stretch

Stand sideways to a chair with your feet together, resting your left arm on the chair back for support. Extend your right arm up and reach for the ceiling. At the same time, allow your body to bow outward and feel the stretch along the right side of your torso and hip. Switch sides and repeat.

8. Hamstring/Side of Back Stretch

Grasp the top of a chair back with both hands, and step backward until you are able to bend forward from the hip at a right angle. As you sink into this position, your feet should be together, and you should feel the stretch in the back of your legs and along both sides of your back. Make sure your back remains straight. If you are too tight at first, bend your elbows and knees slightly. (*Note:* You can segue directly from this stretch to the one that follows by simply opening up your stance.)

9. Inner Thigh/Side of Back Stretch

Stand with your legs about 4 to 5 feet apart and bend forward at the hip, extending your arms straight and resting your forearms on the top of a chair back. You'll feel a stretch along both sides of your back. Now bend your right knee slightly and sink to that side, feeling an additional stretch along the inside of your left thigh. Repeat, bending the left knee.

10. Standing Cat Back/Abdominal Stretch

Keeping your knees slightly bent, bend forward, placing your hands on the seat of a chair to support your torso. Holding your head up, let your stomach sag and arch your back like a cat by tipping your pelvis forward. Then, tighten your abdominals, tip your pelvis up and round your back. Let your head drop as your back comes up. Imagine a string pulling your navel to the ceiling. Hold, then relax.

Chapter 10

Your Strength Training Program

Now that we've covered the basics of strength training, it's time to start lifting! This chapter contains everything you'll need to begin this easy and effective 12-week introduction to lifting weights.

This chapter includes:

The Exercises

Illustrated descriptions of all the exercises in the program are grouped by body part. I've provided an index (pages 100–103) so you can quickly locate a specific exercise by name, or find alternate exercises for a particular body part. This will be especially handy later on if you decide to custom-build your own routine.

The 12-Week Program and Training Log

The Training Log leads you step by step through your first twelve weeks of strength training. All you have to do is read the exercise descriptions for the exercises you're doing on a given week, and begin. You'll find complete instructions for performing the routines and recording your progress at the beginning of the Training Log section.

What to Expect

Once you start the 12-week *Lift Weights to Lose Weight* program, you'll be on your way to discovering a whole new sense of your body and its capabilities. And believe me, these first 12 weeks will be an adventure! Especially if you're new to weight training, you should start to feel changes happening in your body within the first 3 to 4 weeks. By the 12th week, studies show many women are able to double their strength and even begin to see significant improvement in muscle contour. Stick with it through this introductory phase, and I promise you you'll be excited and eager to continue.

At this point, jump to Week One of the routines (page 224), and let's get started!

Chest

Chest Press with Dumbbells *106*
Push-up *108*
Chest Flye *110*

Gym Options
Seated Chest Press Machine *112*
Straight Bar Bench Press *114*

Back

Low Back Extension *118*
One-Arm Row with Dumbbells *120*
High Elbow Row *122*

Gym Options
Lat Pull-down Machine *124*
Cable Low Row *126*

Variety Options
Seated Back Flye *128*
Back Extension with Rotation *130*

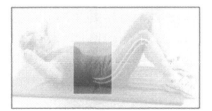

Abdominals

Ab Curl-up *134*
Combo Ab Curl *136*
Assisted Ab Curl-up *138*

Variety Options
Oblique Ab Curl *140*
Reverse Ab Curl *142*

Biceps

Standing Biceps Curl *146*
Biceps Curl with Reverse Grip *148*
Preacher Curl *150*

Gym Options
Cable Curl *152*

Variety Options
Concentration Curl *154*

Triceps

One-Arm Triceps Press *158*
One-Arm French Press *160*
Triceps Dip on Chair *162*

Gym Options
Cable Triceps Pull-down *164*

Shoulders

Lateral Raise *168*
Overhead Press *170*
Rear Raise *172*

Buttocks and Hips

Hip Lift with Legs on Chair *176*
Squat Holding Dumbbells *178*
Skier's Lunge *180*

Gym Options
Leg Press *182*
Leg Extension Machine *184*
Smith Rack Lunge *186*

Variety Options

Front Lunge *188*

Wall Squat with One-Leg Lift *190*

Legs

Self-Resisted Hamstring Curl *194*

Side Lift with Ankle Weights *196*

One-Legged Heel Raise *198*

Gym Options

Leg Curl Machine *200*

Inner/Outer Thigh Machine *202*

Seated Calf Machine *204*

Variety Options

Rear Leg Lift with Ankle Weights *206*

Toe Raise with Self-Resistance *208*

Stabilizer Exercises

Pendulum *212*

Face-Down Plank *214*

Isometric Inner Thigh Squeeze *216*

Face-up Plank *218*

Push-up Position with Leg Lift *220*

One-Leg Lift *222*

Chest

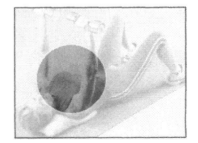

Chest Press with Dumbbells

Targets: Chest (pectoralis major), front of the shoulders (anterior deltoid), back of the upper arms (triceps).

Setup: Lie back on a bench, or on a floor mat with a cushion supporting your shoulders, cradling a pair of dumbbells to the sides of your chest. Keep your feet on the floor or on the end of the bench, your knees raised. Your head, shoulder blades, and buttocks should be in firm contact with the bench or floor.

Move: Holding the weights so that your thumbs face each other and your elbows point to the sides, press the weights up as though you're pressing around a fat barrel. Don't let your dumbbells tilt up or down, and keep the elbows slightly bent at the top of the movement. Then, lower the weight until your upper arms are parallel to the ground. On your last rep, bring your elbows in and cradle the weights back to a safe position at your sides.

Focus: Don't let your back arch. If your bench is too high to allow your feet to rest on the floor and your back to remain flat, put your feet up on the bench. Don't lower your upper arms any deeper than parallel to the floor, and keep your elbows from moving in or out. Avoid rounding the upper back by keeping your shoulder blades pulled together.

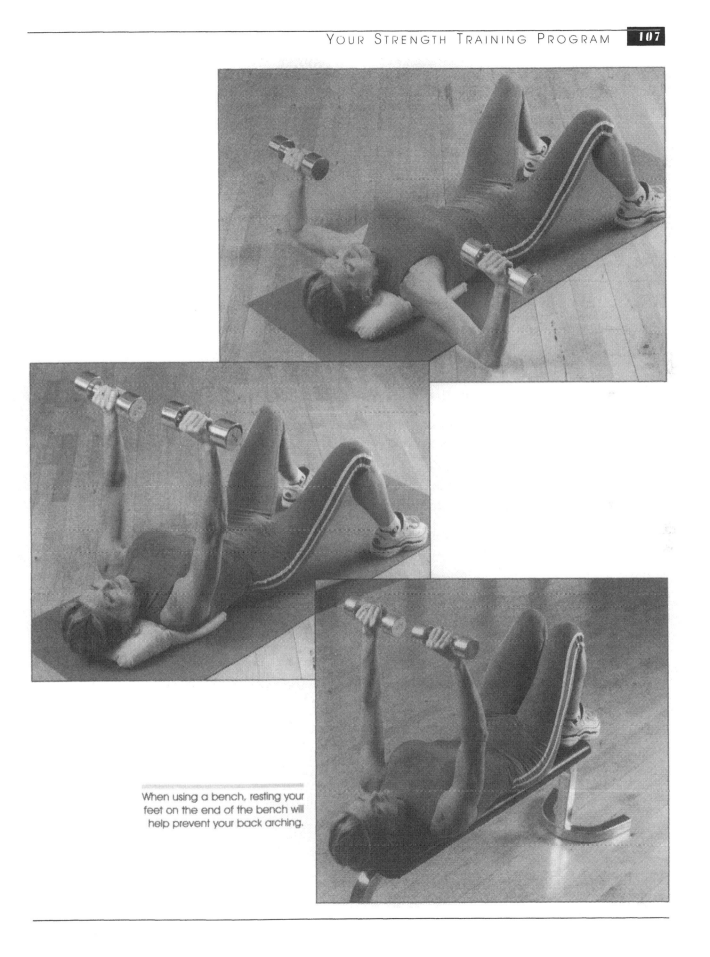

When using a bench, resting your feet on the end of the bench will help prevent your back arching.

Push-up

Targets: Chest (pectoralis major), front of the shoulders (anterior deltoid), and back of the upper arms (triceps).

Setup: Kneel on the ground with your arms lined up so that your wrists are directly beneath your shoulders and fingertips are straight ahead or turned in slightly. Walk your hands forward until your body forms as straight a line as possible from your knees up to your shoulders. Keep your neck in line with your spine.

Move: Inhale, bending your elbows, lowering your body down until your chest nears the floor. Pause, exhale, and press back up to starting position.

Focus: Hold your abdominal muscles in tight so that your body is in a straight line as you lower it. Don't let your back sag as your arms get tired. Keep your shoulders over your wrists the whole time; avoid the tendency to push your weight back when you get tired. If you can't lower your body all the way down, start with a quarter push-up and gradually progress lower. When the kneeling push-up gets easy, straighten out your legs and balance on your toes.

When the kneeling push-up gets too easy, try this straight-legged version, balancing on your toes.

Chest Flye

Targets: Chest (pectoralis major) and front of the shoulders (anterior deltoid).

Setup: Holding a dumbbell in each hand, lie on your back on a bench or on the floor with a firm pillow under your head, shoulders, and upper back. Push your arms straight up until your elbows are almost straight and palms face each other. The dumbbells should be directly above your shoulders and touching.

Move: Inhale, then slowly lower your arms out to the sides, keeping your elbows slightly bent. Continue to lower until your elbows are slightly below your shoulders or you feel a gentle stretch in your chest and shoulder muscles. Pause, exhale, and slowly close your arms back up to starting position.

Focus: Keep your wrists straight, almost as if you were wearing a cast on each one. In the starting position you should feel like you're hugging a big beach ball. As you lower your arms, imagine that the ball is getting bigger, pushing your arms open. To really target the chest, keep your arms in line with your shoulders; at the end of the movement, your body should look like a lowercase *t*.

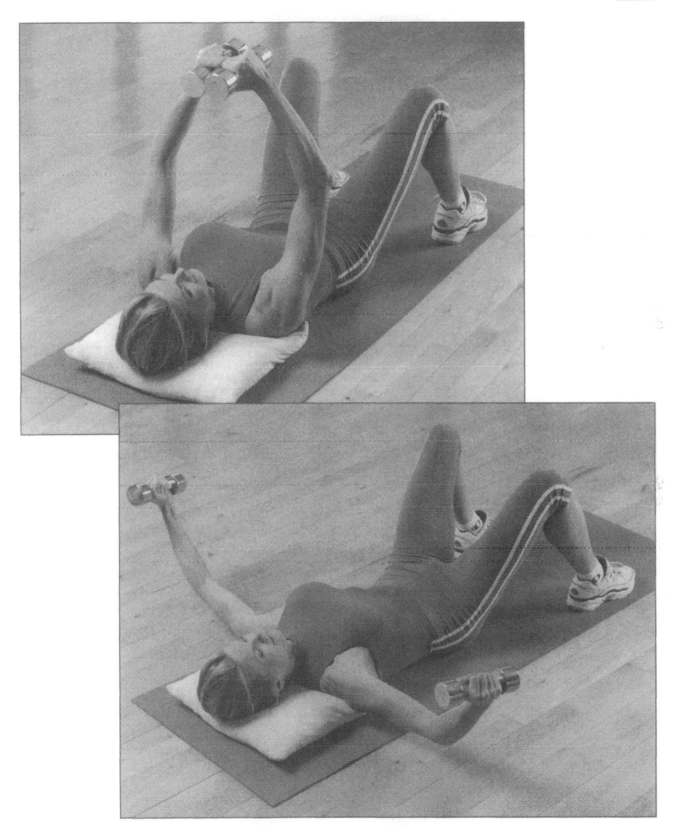

Gym Option: Seated Chest Press Machine
Substitute for Chest Press with Dumbbells

Targets: Chest (pectoralis major), front of the shoulders (anterior deltoid), and back of the upper arms (triceps).

Setup: Sit with your feet flat on the floor or machine platform, and your shoulder blades and head in contact with the padded bench. Adjust the seat so that your elbows are positioned at about shoulder height. Holding the handles, pull your shoulder blades together and try to hold this position throughout the exercise.

Move: Exhale, and press your arms out in front of you until your elbows are almost straight. Pause, inhale, and slowly bring your arms back to the starting position.

Focus: Be careful not to lock your elbows at the end of the pressing movement.

Comments: I have to think hard about keeping my shoulder blades squeezed together during this exercise, but doing so makes the exercise more effective and you'll really feel those chest muscles working.

Use the foot bar to relieve the strain on your arms when getting in and out of the starting position.

Gym Option: Straight Bar Bench Press
Substitute for Push-up

Targets: Chest (pectoralis major), front of the shoulders (anterior deltoid), and back of the upper arms (triceps).

Setup: Lie on your back on a bench with your feet flat on the ground or placed on the end of the bench with knees raised. Hold the bar so that, in the lowered position, you will have a 90-degree angle between your upper and lower arm. Your hands should be about shoulder width apart, or just slightly wider, with the elbows pointing out.

Move: Inhale, and lower the bar to your chest. Then exhale and slowly press the bar straight up away from your chest.

Focus: Maintain a natural arch in your lower back. Don't excessively arch or flatten your back while pressing. Your upper arm should not go deeper than parallel to the floor as you lower the bar.

Comments: If you squeeze the shoulder blades together tightly, and hold them in this position throughout the movement, you will really feel this exercise in the chest.

"Spotting" your partner for safety.

Low Back Extension

Targets: Lower back (erector spinae).

Setup: Lie on your stomach with your feet down and forehead resting on your hands, elbows out to the side.

Move: Keeping your neck straight, exhale, and slowly lift your chest off the floor using your lower back muscles. Pause at the top, inhale, and lower back to starting position. Keep the tops of your feet on the floor—don't kick your legs up into a "Superman" position! That can place excess stress on your lower back.

Focus: Don't lift your head; concentrate on using those back muscles to raise your torso. Keep your eyes focused on the floor and your elbows out to the side. Lift only as high as you comfortably can—even an inch or two is fine.

One-Arm Row with Dumbbells

Targets: Sides of upper back (latissimus dorsi, trapezius), back of the shoulder (posterior deltoid), front of the upper arm (biceps).

Setup: Place your left knee on the edge of a chair or on a bench with the left hip directly over it. The knee of your right leg should be at the same height and slightly bent. Support yourself with your left hand by gripping the end of the bench. Your upper body should be parallel to the floor. Lower your body to pick up the weight in your right hand. Let your arm hang down with the elbow slightly bent, tucked in close to your side. Pull your shoulder blades together and keep them together throughout the exercise.

Move: Bend your right arm at the elbow and pull the weight up until the upper arm is parallel to the floor (or a little beyond) and the elbow forms a right angle. Pause and slowly return to the starting position. Switch arms after each set.

Focus: Keep the weight close to your side throughout the lift. Maintain normal curves in your neck and lower back, and keep your head level.

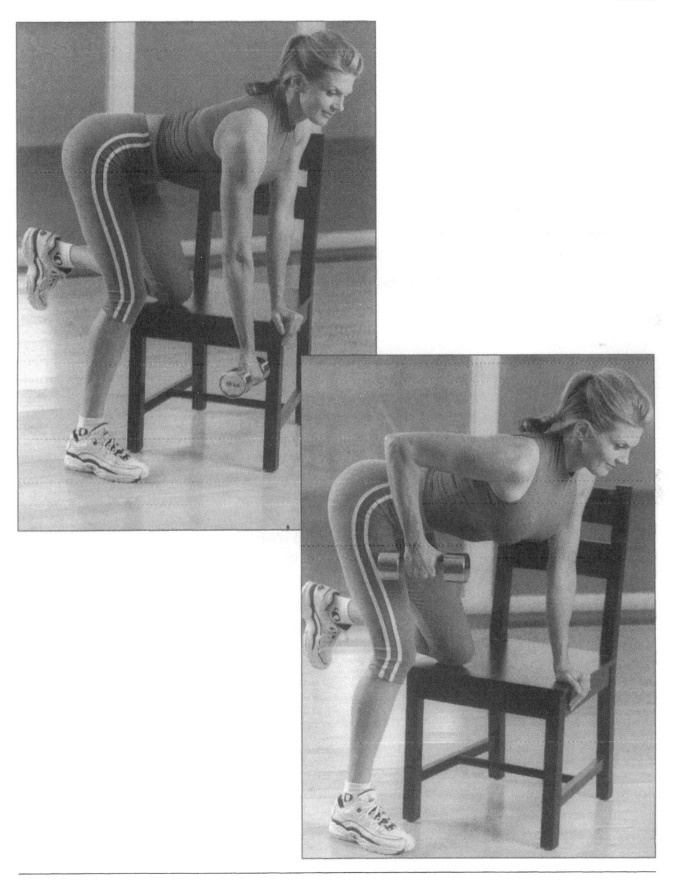

High Elbow Row

Targets: Upper back (trapezius, rhomboids), back of the shoulders (posterior deltoid), and front of the upper arms (biceps).

Setup: Sit on a chair with a pillow on your lap and lean forward, letting your chest rest on the pillow. With a dumbbell in each hand, let your arms hang down to the sides of your body, palms facing back.

Move: Exhale, and slowly bend your arms, pointing your elbows out to the sides. Lift until your elbows are in line with your shoulders, making sure your palms keep facing back. Pause at the top of the movement, inhale, and lower back down.

Focus: Squeeze your shoulder blades together throughout the movement. Try to keep your head in line with your spine, rather than looking up or down.

Comments: Strong muscles in your upper back and rear shoulders are important to help maintain good posture. Good posture will make you look and feel more fit.

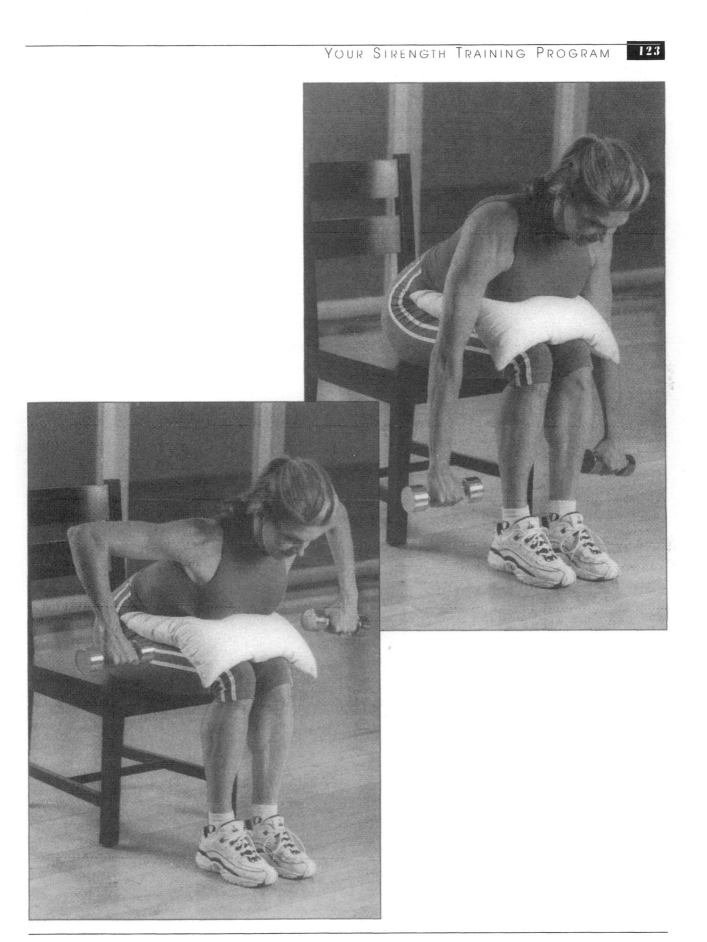

Gym Option: Lat Pull-down Machine
Substitute for Low Back Extension

Targets: Back of the shoulders (posterior deltoid), large muscles in the sides of the back (latissimus dorsi), and front of the upper arm (biceps).

Setup: Place your hands on the bar and sit with your knees under the pad. Lean back slightly without rounding your back.

Move: Pull your shoulder blades down and back. Holding this position, exhale, bend the elbows, and begin to pull the arms out and down until your elbows are at your sides. Hold for a moment, inhale, then return slowly to starting position.

Focus: Don't let your lower back excessively arch or round as you pull down. Keep your elbows pointing toward the ground in order to avoid stress on the shoulders and work the muscles more effectively.

Comments: This is a great exercise to help reshape the upper back and improve your posture.

Gym Option: Cable Low Row
Substitute for High Elbow Row

Targets: Upper back (rhomboids, trapezius), sides of the back (latissimus dorsi), back of the shoulders (posterior deltoid), and front of the upper arms (biceps).

Setup: Sit up straight, bend your knees slightly, and place your feet against the foot rests or on the floor. Grip a V-bar handle with your palms facing in and your elbows slightly bent. Pull your shoulder blades together and hold this position throughout the exercise.

Move: Exhale and bend your elbows, pulling the handle toward your waist. Keep your upper arms close to your sides and your elbows pointing down. When your elbows are under or slightly behind your shoulders, pause and inhale, then return slowly to the starting position.

Focus: This exercise can be tricky because you have to keep your torso upright as you row. Don't bend forward or lean back as your arms are moving.

Comments: This Cable Low Row is not only good for strengthening the back muscles, it's also a great posture exercise. You'll improve your posture by holding your back in the upright position and squeezing your shoulder blades.

Variety Option: Seated Back Flye

Substitute for any exercise for this body part

Targets: Upper back (trapezius) and rear of the shoulders (posterior deltoid).

Setup: Sit on a chair with a pillow on your lap and lean forward, letting your chest rest on the pillow. Grasping your lightest dumbbells, let your arms hang down to the sides.

Move: Exhale, squeeze your shoulder blades together, and slowly lift your arms out to the side until they're slightly higher than shoulder level. Pause, inhale, and lower back down.

Focus: Make sure your arms lift directly out to the side, not behind you. Keep your shoulder blades squeezed when you lift the weights *and* when you lower them. Release your shoulder blades at the bottom of the movement.

Comments: It's a good idea to practice this exercise a few times with no weight. When you do begin to use weights, use your lightest dumbbells at first.

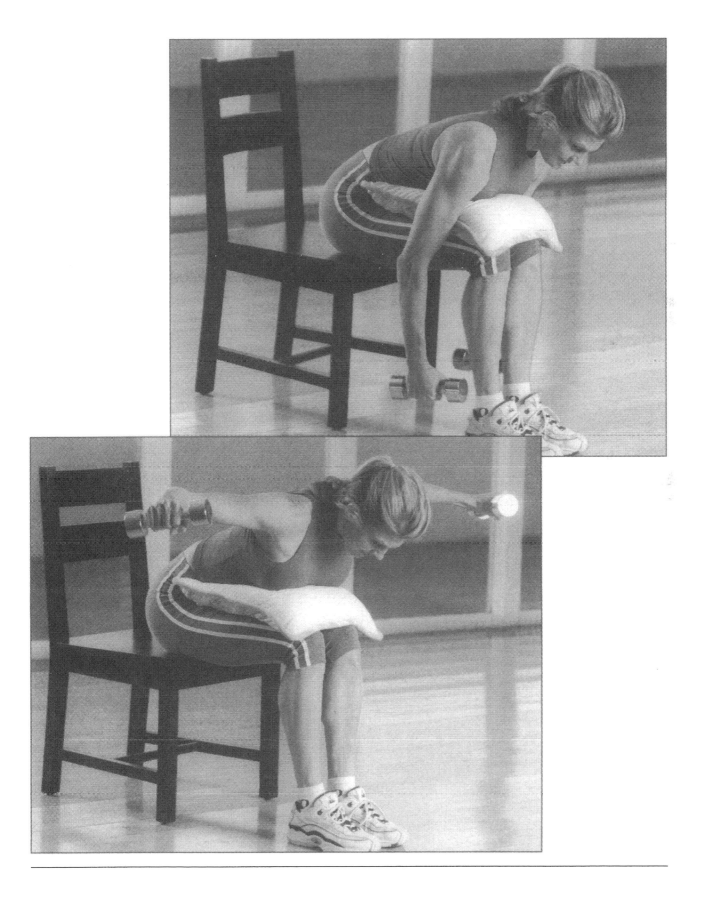

Variety Option: Back Extension With Rotation

Substitute for any exercise for this body part

Targets: Lower back (erector spinae).

Setup: Lie on your stomach with feet down, forehead resting on your hands, and elbows out to the sides.

Move: This is a four-count movement: 1) Exhale, and lift your chest off the floor. 2) Twist your torso to the right until your left elbow touches the floor and your right elbow points diagonally toward the ceiling. 3) Return to center. 4) Inhale, and lower back down. Alternate sides until you've completed the recommended number of repetitions for each side.

Focus: Let your lower back muscles do all the work. As you twist from your torso, don't rotate your neck; just let your head go along for the ride naturally. Don't let your feet lift off the ground.

Abdominals

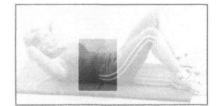

Ab Curl-up

Targets: Abdominals.

Setup: Lie on your back with your knees bent and feet flat on the floor. Place your hands behind your head, and keep your neck relaxed; don't push your chin up or pull it down into your chest. Keep your elbows comfortably out to the side.

Movement: Exhale, tighten your abdominals, and pull your rib cage toward your hips, lifting your head, neck, and shoulder blades off the ground as one unit. Remember: This isn't an old-fashioned sit-up—you don't need to lift more than a couple of inches off the floor. Pause at the top of the movement, then inhale as you slowly lower all the way back down.

Focus: Concentrate on pulling your rib cage down, as opposed to lifting your head and shoulders up. Make sure the movement comes from your abs—not your neck or shoulders. Use your hands only to support your head, not lift it.

Combo Ab Curl

Targets: Upper and lower regions of abdominals.

Setup: Lie on your back with your knees lined up directly over your hips. Place your hands behind your head, and keep your neck relaxed. Don't push your chin up or pull it down into your chest.

Move: Exhale, tighten your abdominals, and pull your rib cage toward your hips, lifting your head, neck, and shoulder blades off the ground as one unit. Simultaneously, curl your hips off the floor. Pause at the top of the move, then inhale and lower back down.

Focus: Concentrate on pulling your ribs and hips toward one another. Make sure the movement comes from your abs, rather than using momentum to swing your hips and shoulders up.

Comments: The combo curl offers a good challenge: to smoothly combine a curl-up and a reverse curl. You may want to practice a couple reps of each first before combining them.

Assisted Ab Curl-up

Targets: Abdominals.

Setup: Lie on your back with your knees bent and feet flat on the floor. Place your hands behind your head, and keep your neck relaxed. Don't push your chin up or pull it down into your chest.

Move: This is a three-part exercise. Part 1: Exhale and curl up, pulling your rib cage down toward your hips. Hold at the top of the movement. Part 2: Reach forward and place your hands around the backs of your thighs. Use your arms to pull yourself a little higher. Part 3: Let go of your legs and hold the higher position for a second or two. Inhale, and slowly lower all the way back down.

Focus: Make sure all the effort comes from your abs, not your neck or shoulders. Slow, controlled movement is much more effective than fast movement that uses momentum.

Comments: I like this exercise because you get a great stretch in the back muscles while you're strengthening your abs.

Variety Option: Oblique Ab Curl
Substitute for any exercise for this body part

Targets: Front and side abdominals.

Setup: Lie on your back with your knees bent and feet flat on the floor. Place your hands behind your head, elbows comfortably out to the side, and keep your neck relaxed, as in the Curl-up.

Move: Exhale. As you curl your head, neck, and shoulder blades off the floor, rotate your torso, pulling the left side of your rib cage toward your right inner thigh. Pause at the top, inhale, and slowly lower back down. You can do all of your repetitions on one side before switching sides, or you can alternate sides throughout each set. Be sure to do the recommended number of repetitions for each side.

Focus: Make sure you rotate only your torso—not your arms and neck. Keep your elbows in line with your ears throughout the movement. Concentrate on pulling your rib cage down and across rather than pulling your elbows across.

Variety Option: **Reverse Ab Curl**
Substitute for any exercise for this body part

Targets: Lower portion of abdominals.

Setup: Lie on your back with your knees lined up directly over your hips. Your heels should hang down near the back of your thighs. Rest your arms on the floor beside you, palms facing down.

Move: Exhale, tighten your abdominals, and tilt your hips off the floor. Pause at the top of the move, inhale, and lower back down. This is a subtle move—your hips barely need to clear the floor.

Focus: Concentrate on lifting with the lower part of your abdominal muscles, not your front hip muscles. Don't kick or swing your legs. Try not to push on the floor with your hands; if you're tempted, place your hands behind your head.

Biceps

Standing Biceps Curl

Targets: Front of the upper arms (biceps).

Setup: Stand up straight with feet shoulder width apart, and your weight evenly centered between toes and heels. Hold a dumbbell in each hand with your arms hanging at your sides.

Move: Exhale, and slowly bend your elbows, curling the dumbbells up to your shoulders. As you bend your arms, rotate your wrists outward, and keep your wrists a little wider than the elbows. At the top of the movement, your palms are facing your shoulders. Inhale and slowly lower back down.

Focus: Don't let the weight of the dumbbells pull your wrists into a bent position. Tighten your abs to help you maintain perfect upright posture.

Comments: It's easy to swing your arms from the shoulders as you curl. I like to think about keeping my elbows close to my sides and my shoulders pulled down away from my ears.

Biceps Curl with Reverse Grip

Targets: Front of the upper arms (biceps).

Setup: Stand up straight with feet shoulder width apart, and your weight evenly centered between toes and heels. Hold a dumbbell in each hand with your arms hanging by your sides, palms facing back.

Move: Exhale, and slowly bend your elbows, curling the dumbbells up toward your shoulders. As you bend your arms, keep your wrists a little wider than the elbows. At the top of the movement, your palms are facing down. Inhale and slowly lower back down.

Focus: Don't let the weight of the dumbbells pull your wrists into a bent position. Tighten your abs to help you maintain perfect upright posture.

Comments: It's easy to swing your arms from the shoulders as you curl. I like to think about keeping my elbows close to my sides and my shoulders pulled down away from my ears.

Preacher Curl

Targets: Front of the upper arms (biceps).

Setup: Sit on a chair with a pillow on your lap and lean forward, letting your chest rest on the pillow. With a dumbbell in each hand, place your arms across the pillow with your elbows just above your knees. Your palms are facing forward or up.

Move: Exhale, and bend your elbows, curling the dumbbells up to your shoulders. Keep your wrists straight. Pause at the top of the movement, inhale, and slowly lower back down.

Focus: Keep your abs tight and back extended throughout the movement. Don't slump forward or round your shoulders.

Comments: If you have a tendency to want to swing your arms when doing biceps curls, this is a good exercise for you. The preacher curl position will keep your arms still and stable.

Gym Option: Cable Curl
Substitute for Biceps Curl with Reverse Grip

Targets: Front of the upper arms (biceps).

Setup: Stand close to the cable machine with your feet about shoulder width apart and knees slightly bent. Grasp the bar with your palms facing up and the hands placed slightly wider than shoulder width apart. Pull your upper arms to the sides of your body, with your elbows near your waist.

Move: Exhale and bend your elbows, pulling the bar up toward your chest. Hold, inhale, and slowly return to the starting position.

Focus: Try not to move your upper arm at all while curling your lower arm up. Avoid bending forward or leaning back as you perform the curl.

Comments: It's easy to swing your arms using your shoulder and back muscles to cheat on this exercise. Try to keep everything except your lower arms still and stable.

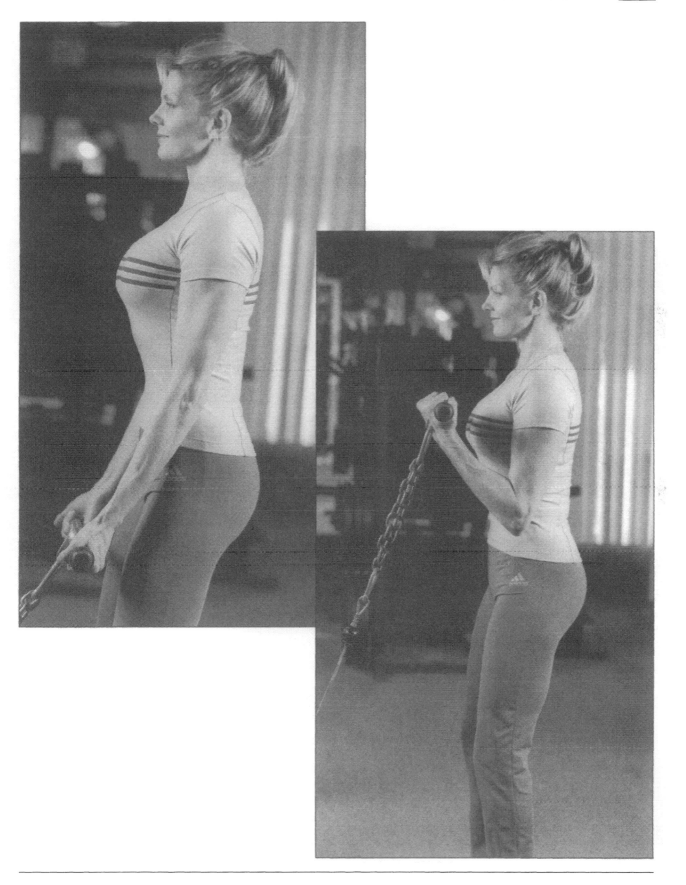

Variety Option: Concentration Curl
Substitute for any exercise for this body part

Targets: Front of the upper arm (biceps).

Setup: Sit on the corner of a chair with legs apart, lean forward, and let your left palm rest on your left knee. Holding a dumbbell in your right hand, rest the back of your right arm against the inside of your right thigh. Your right palm should face your left ankle.

Move: Exhale, slowly bend your right elbow, and gradually rotate your palm so it faces your shoulder at the top of the movement.

Focus: Curl the weight as high as you can, squeezing your biceps at the top of the move. Lift and lower the weight at the same speed.

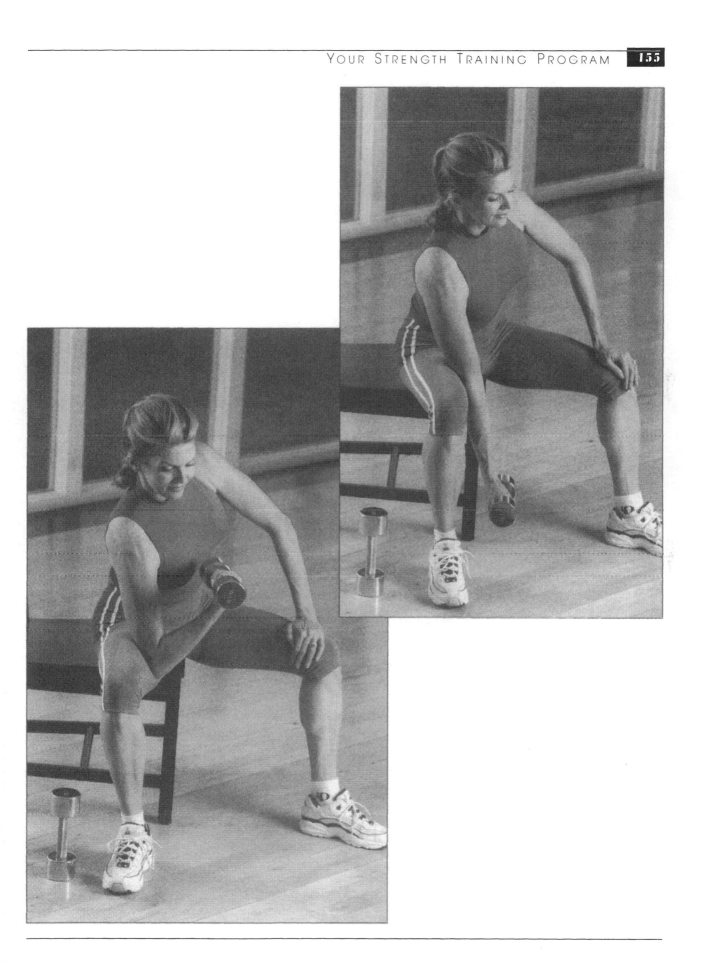

Triceps

One-Arm Triceps Press

Targets: Back of the upper arm (triceps).

Setup: Lean forward, place your left hand on the seat of a chair, and stagger your feet so your left leg is in front of your right and both knees are slightly bent. Holding a dumbbell in your right hand, lift your arm until your elbow is slightly higher than your body and the dumbbell is parallel to the floor, palm facing in.

Move: Exhale, then slowly straighten your elbow until your arm is straight and dumbbell points to the floor. Pause at the top of the movement, inhale, and return to starting position.

Focus: Throughout the exercise, keep your upper arm still, your back straight, and both shoulders facing the floor.

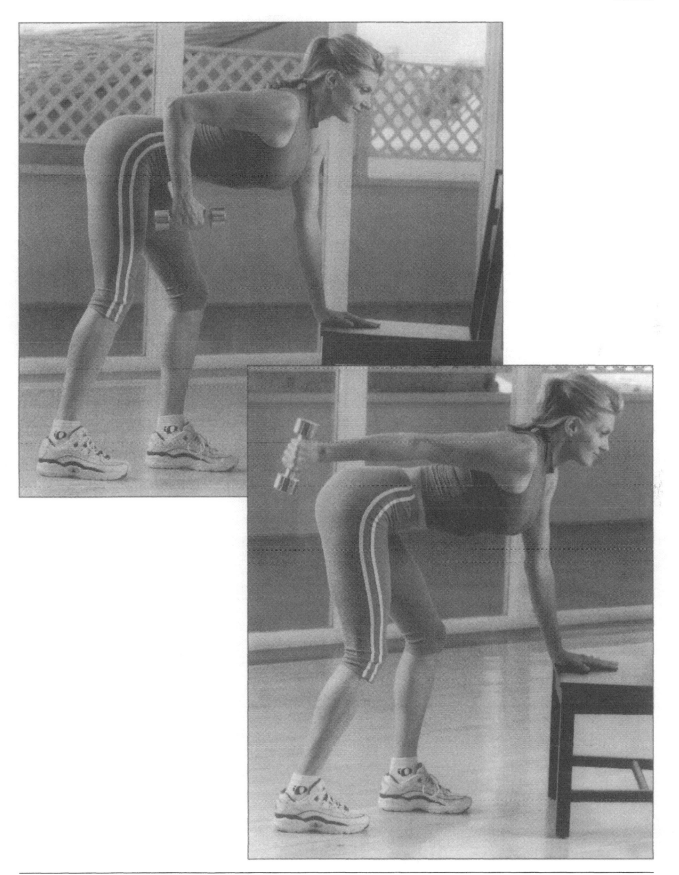

One-Arm French Press

Targets: Back of the upper arm (triceps).

Setup: Sit on a chair with your back straight and feet flat on the floor. Holding a dumbbell in one hand, lift the arm straight up and slightly in front of your head. Place your other hand slightly above your elbow to brace the arm in this lifted position.

Move: Exhale and slowly bend your elbow, lowering the dumbbell until it almost touches your shoulder. Pause at the bottom of the movement, inhale, and straighten your elbow back up to your starting position.

Focus: Try to keep your upper arm pointed up, rather than forward. Don't let your elbow drift as you lower and lift the dumbbell.

Comments: I like this exercise because it's so focused. You'll really feel the triceps working—if you concentrate on perfect technique!

Triceps Dip on Chair

Targets: Back of the upper arms (triceps).

Setup: Sit on the edge of a chair with heels on the floor about six inches beyond your knees. Place your hands on the corners or side edges of the chair, with your thumbs pointing front. Keeping your arms straight, shift your weight forward until your hips just clear the front of the chair.

Move: Exhale, and bend your elbows until your upper arms are almost level with your shoulders. Keep your elbows pointing back and your hips and lower back close to the chair. Pause at the bottom of the movement, inhale, and press back up.

Focus: Press your shoulder blades down throughout the exercise. Don't lower any deeper than the point at which your upper arms are parallel to the floor.

Comments: The dip is great for your triceps, but if you have wrist problems, you may want to substitute one of the other triceps exercises in place of this chair dip.

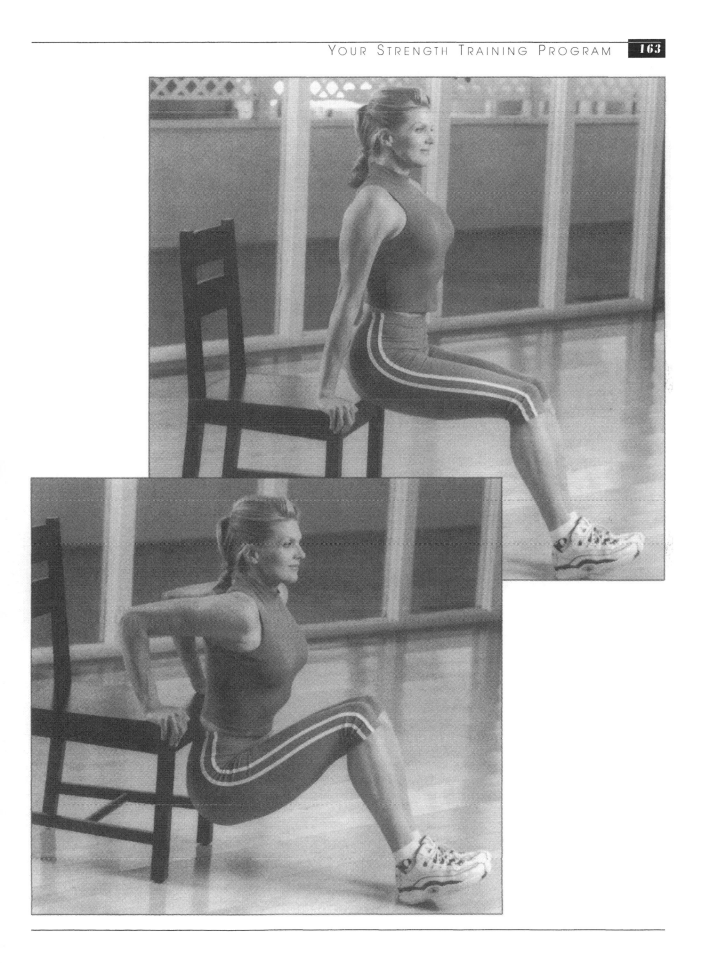

Gym Option: Cable Triceps Pull-down
Substitute for Triceps Dip on Chair

Targets: Back of the upper arm (triceps).

Setup: Stand close to the cable machine with your feet about shoulder width apart and knees slightly bent. Grasp the bar with your palms facing down, and pull your arms in close to the sides of your body with slightly bent elbows. Your hands should be about shoulder width apart.

Move: Inhale and slowly bend your elbows, letting your forearms come toward your chest until your forearms are at a 90 degree angle to your body. Pause, exhale, and press your arms back down to the starting position.

Focus: Keep your upper arms firmly in place as you press your lower arms down.

Comments: This is a good exercise to target the triceps muscles, but you have to keep the shoulders and upper arms really still for the best isolation.

Shoulders

Lateral Raise

Target: Center shoulder muscles (lateral deltoid).

Setup: Stand with your feet slightly apart, knees slightly bent, abdominals tightened, and arms hanging by your sides. Hold a dumbbell in each hand, palms facing in.

Move: Exhale, and slowly lift your arms out to the side until the dumbbells are slightly higher than your shoulders. Pause, inhale, and slowly lower back down.

Focus: Lift directly out to the side; don't let the dumbbells end up in front of your thighs. At the top of the movement, let your thumbs turn slightly upward. Keep your elbows slightly bent, not locked.

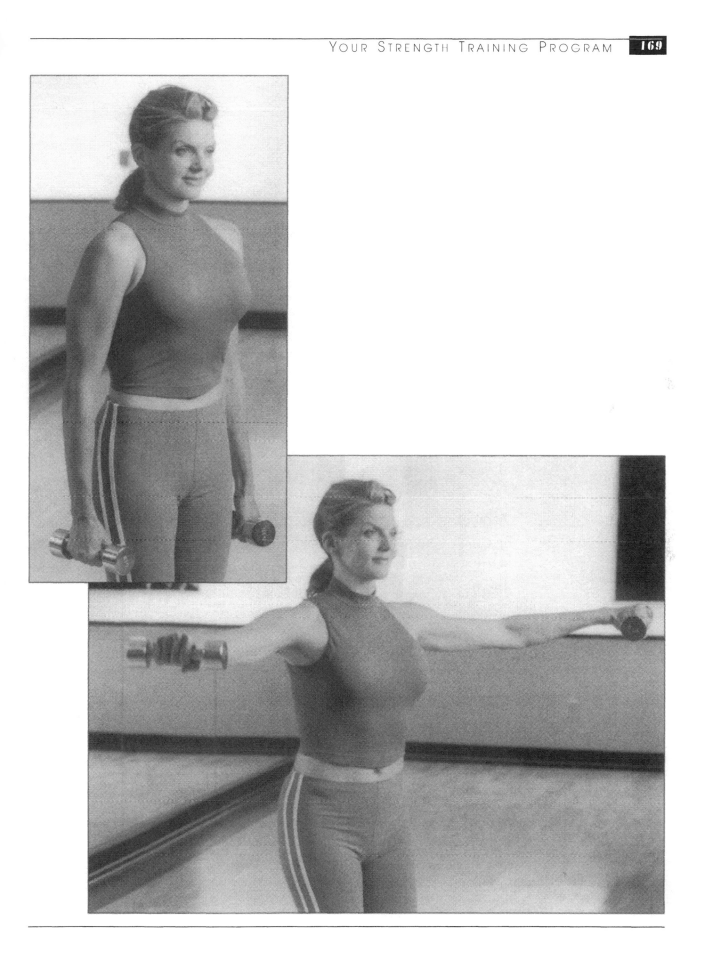

Overhead Press

Targets: Shoulders (lateral deltoid), back of the upper arms (triceps), and the upper back/neck area (upper trapezius).

Setup: Sit on a chair with your back straight and your feet flat on the floor about a foot apart. Hold a dumbbell in each hand, letting them rest on your upper thighs. Raise the dumbbells to shoulder height with your elbows bent and pointing out to the sides and your palms facing front.

Move: Exhale, and straighten your arms, pushing the dumbbells over and slightly in front of your head. Pause, inhale, and lower slowly back to starting position.

Focus: Keep your head level and maintain the natural curves of your lower back. Avoid arching the back as you press the arms overhead. Don't try to press the weights directly over your head. Leaning slightly back into the chair, and pressing slightly forward with the arms, will help protect your shoulders.

Comments: This exercise is simple to perform and can give you great shape and definition in your shoulders.

Rear Raise

Targets: Rear shoulders (posterior deltoid) and back of the upper arms (triceps).

Setup: Stand with your feet hip width apart, knees slightly bent, abdominals tightened, and arms hanging by your sides. Hold a dumbbell in each hand, palms facing in.

Move: Exhale, and, keeping your arms straight, lift your arms behind you as high as you can. Pause, exhale, and slowly lower back down. Keep your palms facing in.

Focus: As you lift your arms back, try not to lean forward. Keep your body upright. Don't let your arms flare out to the side; lift them directly behind you.

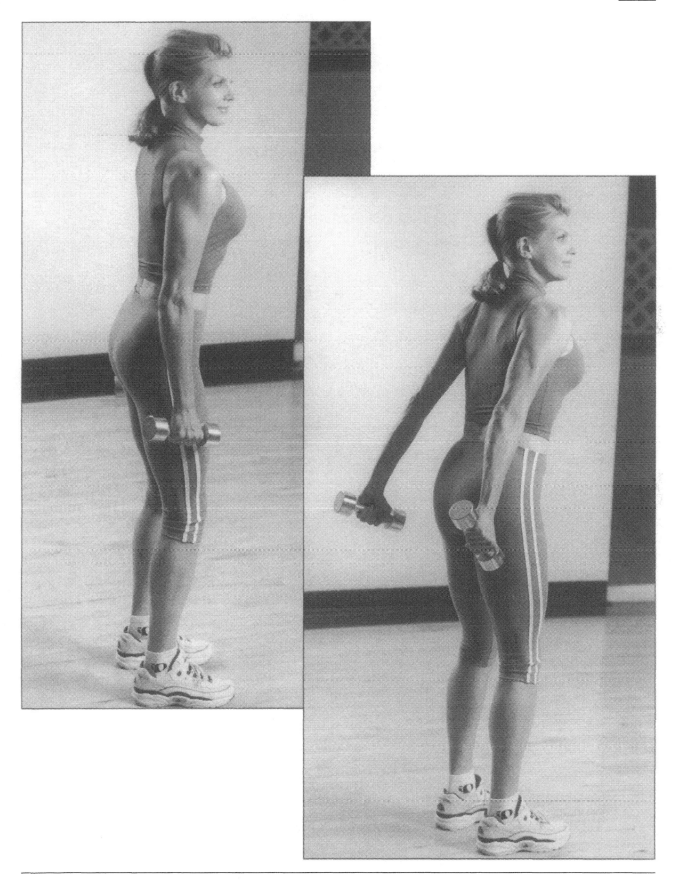

Buttocks and Hips

Hip Lift with Legs on Chair

Targets: Buttocks (gluteals) and back of the thighs (hamstrings).

Setup: Lie on your back on the floor with your heels resting on the seat of a chair and your knees slightly bent. Rest your arms on the floor slightly away from your body.

Move: Exhale. Press your heels into the chair, tense your buttocks, and lift your body up until it forms a straight line from your shoulders to your heels. Pause, inhale, and slowly lower yourself back down.

Focus: Lift at a slow, controlled speed instead of throwing your body up into the air. Keep your back straight, not arched. Make sure you feel the weight across your shoulders, not on your head or the back of your neck.

Squat Holding Dumbbells

Targets: Front and rear thigh muscles (quadriceps, hamstrings) and buttocks (gluteals).

Setup: Stand up straight with your abdominals tightened and your feet hip width apart. I like to cross my arms in front of my chest and rest the dumbbells on my shoulders. If you prefer, you can let your arms hang straight down.

Move: Inhale, bend your knees as if you're going to sit in a chair, and lower down until your thighs are nearly parallel to the floor. Meanwhile, lift your arms out in front of you for balance. Pause, exhale, and slowly stand up.

Focus: As you lower yourself, make sure your tailbone points back. Keep your chest lifted and back straight, not rounded. Finally, don't let your knees shoot out past your toes.

It's a good idea to practice squats without dumbbells to perfect your form. Here's the ending position for a squat without dumbbells.

Skier's Lunge

Targets: Hips and thighs (quadriceps, hamstrings, gluteals).

Setup: Stand about three feet in front of a chair and place the front of one foot on the seat of the chair, keeping the knee bent slightly. Hold dumbbells with your arms hanging straight down at your sides. Align your shoulders and hips over the heel of your standing leg.

Move: Inhale, bend your front leg, and lower into a lunge. Keep your body upright and allow the back knee to bend a little deeper. Pause at the bottom of the movement, exhale, and press back up.

Focus: Keep your front knee more over your ankle while you lunge, rather than forward of the toes.

Comments: I love this exercise because it strengthens your entire lower body and develops your balance. If you do any type of skiing or skating sports, this exercise is for you, too!

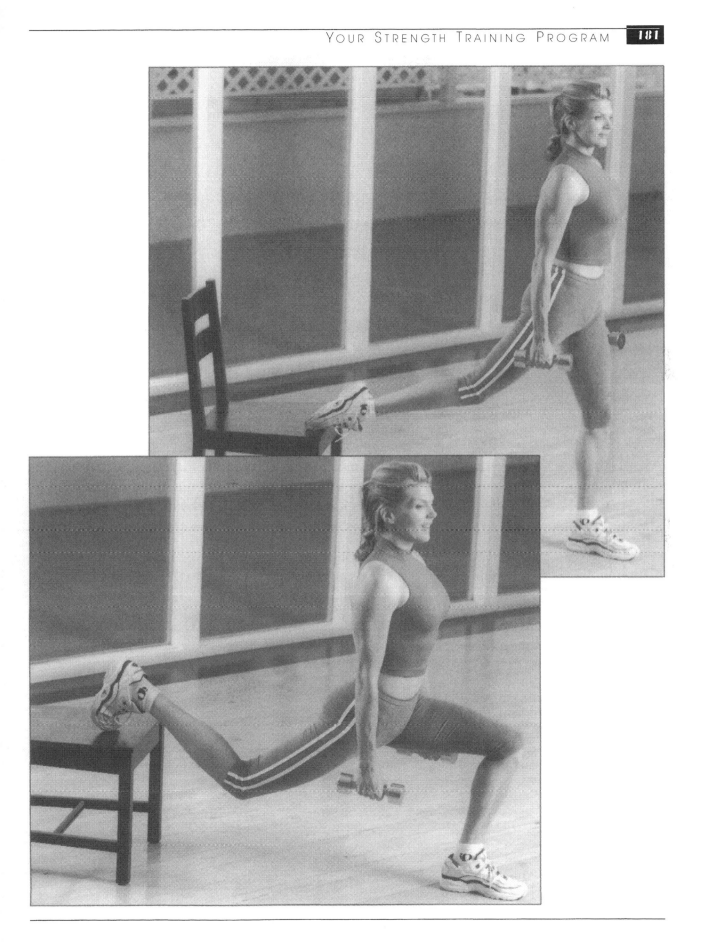

Gym Option: Leg Press
Substitute for Hip Lift with Legs on Chair

Targets: Hips (gluteals), front of the thighs (quadriceps), and back of the thighs (hamstrings).

Setup: Lean back in the machine with your shoulder blades and head resting against the backpad. Keep a natural arch in the low back. Position your feet on the footrest so that your heels are lined up with your knees. Adjust the machine so that your knees are bent about 90 degrees in this starting position. Your feet should be about hip width apart.

Move: Exhale, and push your legs away from you until your knees are almost straight. Hold, inhale, and slowly return to the starting position.

Focus: Keep a natural arch in the lower back. Avoid rounding or hyper-extending as you press. Try not to go any deeper than the point where the upper and lower legs form a 90 degree angle.

Comments: This is a *compound* exercise that works more muscles overall than many other isolated hip and leg exercises. That means more bang for your buck!

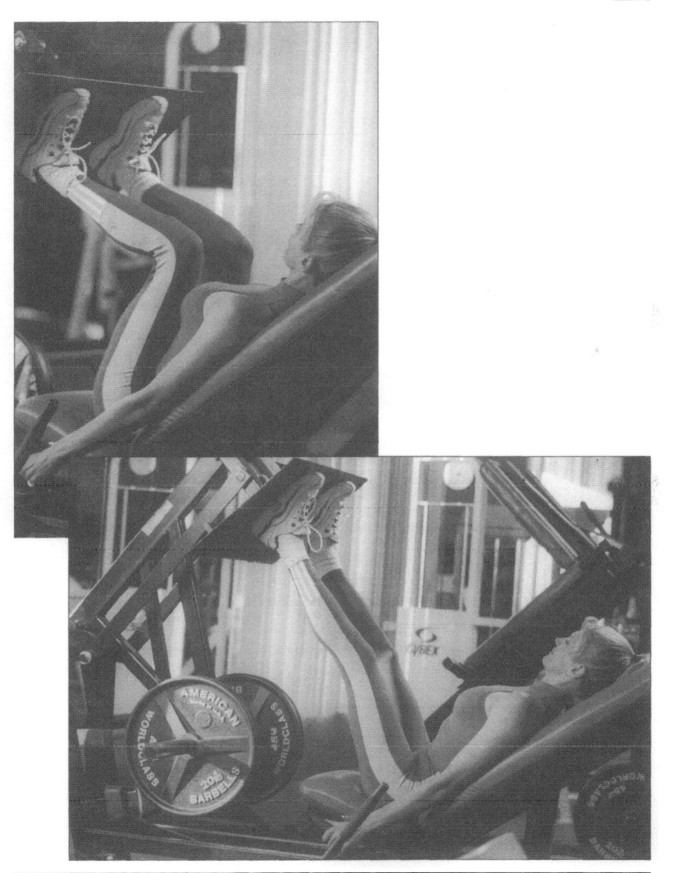

Gym Option: Leg Extension Machine
Substitute for Squat Holding Dumbbells

Targets: Front of the thighs (quadriceps).

Setup: Sit in the machine with your hips and back pressed firmly against the back pad. Adjust the seat so that your knees are lined up with the pivoting point of the machine arm, and adjust the leg pad so that it rests just above your feet. The machine should also be adjusted so that you begin with your knees bent no more than 90 degrees.

Move: Exhale, and begin to straighten your knees. Keep lifting the pad until your knees are a few degrees shy of straight. Pause, inhale, and slowly lower back to the starting position.

Focus: Keep a natural arch in your lower back. Don't excessively arch as you straighten your legs. As you lower, your legs should stop at the point where your upper and lower leg form a 90 degree angle.

Comments: Here's another muscle group that's hard to isolate with little or no equipment. I love how this exercise makes my quads feel.

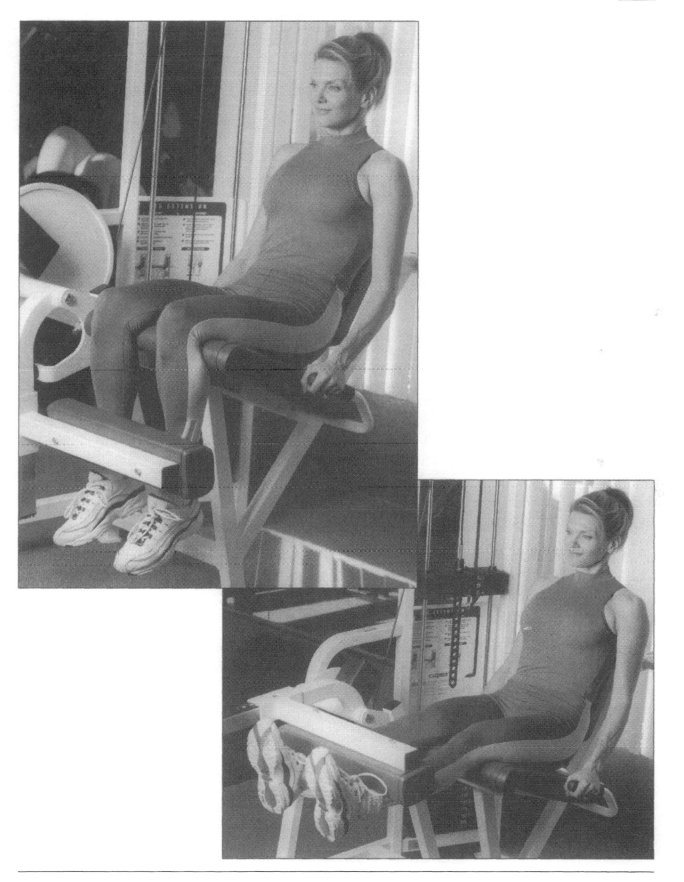

Gym Option: Smith Rack Lunge
Substitute for Skier's Lunge

Targets: Hips (gluteals), back of the thighs (hamstrings), and front of the thighs (quadriceps).

Setup: Stand with one foot approximately two to three feet behind the other in a lunge position. Your front foot should be slightly in front of your shoulders. The bar should rest across your upper back and shoulders. Bend your knees slightly.

Move: Inhale and bend the knees slowly, lowering your body until the forward thigh is approximately parallel to the floor and the rear knee is a few inches from the floor. Pause, exhale, and press back up to the starting position.

Focus: Keep the hips facing forward. Make sure your stance is wide enough that your front knee is above your shoelaces, rather than over the toes.

Comments: This exercise requires a lot of concentration to maintain proper alignment. Go slowly and really focus on your technique.

Variety Option: Front Lunge
Substitute for any exercise for this body part

Targets: Buttocks (gluteals), front and back of the thighs (quadriceps, hamstrings).

Setup: Stand up straight with your abdominals tightened, arms hanging by your sides holding dumbbells, and feet together.

Move: Inhale, and take a large step forward with your right leg, keeping your arms by your sides. Bend both knees so your right knee is directly over your right ankle and your left knee points to the floor with your heel lifted. Your right thigh should be parallel to the floor. Exhale, and push off your right toes back to the starting position. Alternate legs.

Focus: Throughout each repetition, keep slightly more weight on your front leg. If you have trouble balancing, practice the movement without weights, placing a chair at your side and grasping it lightly with one hand.

Variety Option: Wall Squat with One-Leg Lift
Substitute for any exercise for this body part

Targets: Hips and thighs (gluteals, quadriceps, hamstrings) as stabilizers.

Setup: Stand upright with your back leaning against a wall. Walk your feet out about 2 feet from the wall and plant your feet together flat on the floor. Slide your back down the wall until your hips are level with or slightly higher than your knees. In this position, your knees should be above your ankles and your back firmly pressed against the wall.

Move: Exhale, tighten your abdominals, and lift one leg a few inches off the floor. Hold and balance in this position for 5 to 15 seconds. Lower the foot back to the floor and slide back up the wall to a standing position. Repeat on the other leg.

Focus: Keeping your abs pulled in and your head and shoulders level will really help your balance. Don't be discouraged if you are only able to lift the foot for a second or two at first.

Comments: Make sure you keep breathing as you balance in this wall squat. I try to think calm thoughts and breathe deeply as my muscles (and balance!) are challenged. If you find it too difficult at first to balance on one foot, practice the exercise without the leg lift.

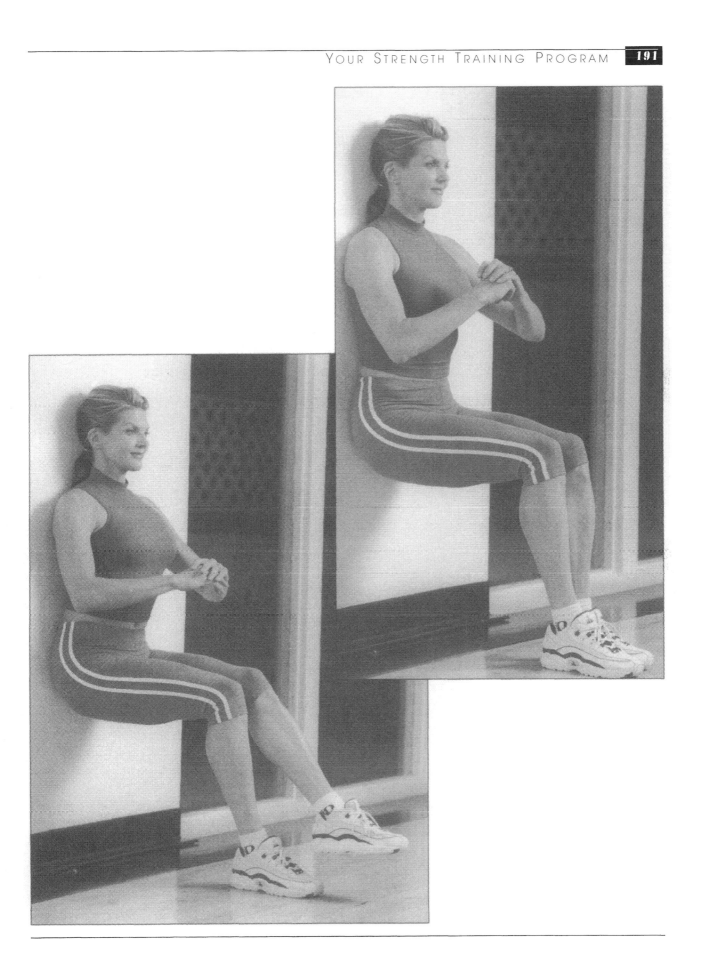

Legs

Self-Resisted Hamstring Curl

Targets: Back of the thighs (hamstrings).

Setup: Lie face-down on the floor with your toes tucked under and your forehead or chin resting on your hands, elbows out to the side. Bend your left knee and place the toes of your left foot on top of the right heel.

Move: Press down with your left foot against your right heel. Exhale, and slowly curl your right leg up as far as you can. Pause, then continue pressing down with your left leg as you lower your right leg back to the floor.

Focus: Keep tension on the bottom leg throughout the movement by pressing down with the top leg. You should feel even resistance through the entire range of motion. Increase the pressure of your top leg as you get stronger.

Comments: This is a great back-of-the-thigh exercise because you can do it anywhere, without equipment. Your own body provides all the resistance you need!

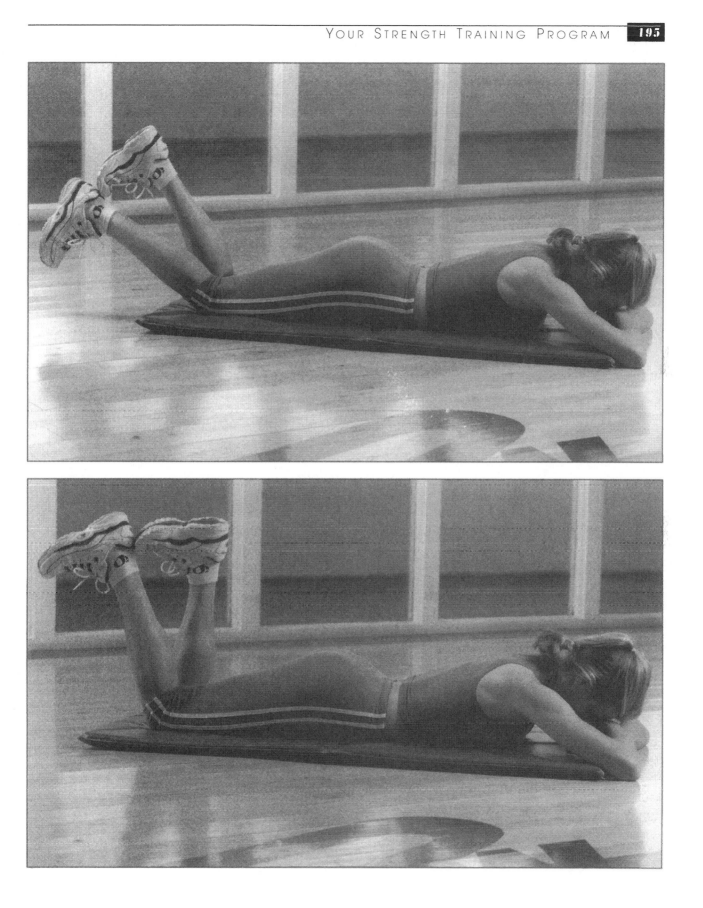

Side Lift with Ankle Weights

Targets: Outer hip muscles (abductors).

Setup: Affix ankle weights to both ankles. Stand up straight with your abdominals tightened and your left side facing the back of a chair. Lean slightly to the side, resting your left elbow on the chair. Place your right hand on your hip.

Move: Exhale, and slowly lift your right leg out to the side, keeping your knee and foot facing forward. Lift as high as you can without turning your knee and toe up to the ceiling.

Focus: Make sure your leg is lifting directly out to the side, not behind you. Your supporting leg muscles are working to keep you balanced and upright.

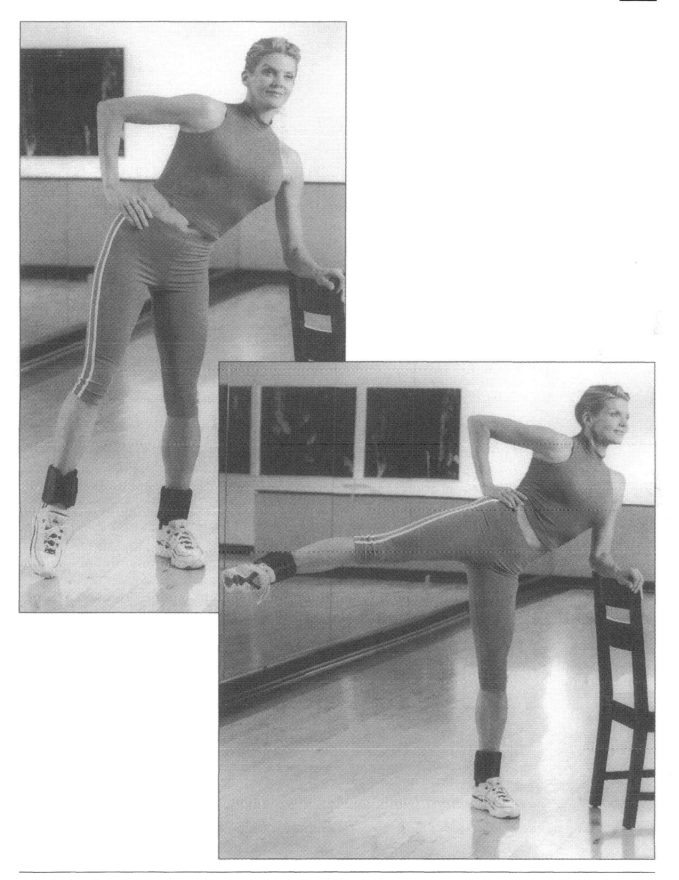

One-Legged Heel Raise

Targets: Calf muscles (gastrocnemius, soleus).

Setup: Stand on a sturdy platform facing the back of a chair, and rest both hands on the seat back for balance. Balance on the ball of one foot, with your heel hanging off the edge of the platform. Bend the other knee about 45 degrees.

Move: Inhale, and slowly lower your heel until you feel a gentle stretch in your calf muscles. Exhale, and push up onto the ball of your foot, lifting your heel as high as you can. Pause at the top, inhale, and lower back down.

Focus: As you lift, keep equal weight across all five toes. Counteract the tendency to roll your foot outward by pressing the big-toe side of your foot into the floor. To keep your balance, pull your abdominal muscles in and keep your buttocks tucked. Lift and lower at the same speed, taking two slow counts in each direction. Repeat with other leg.

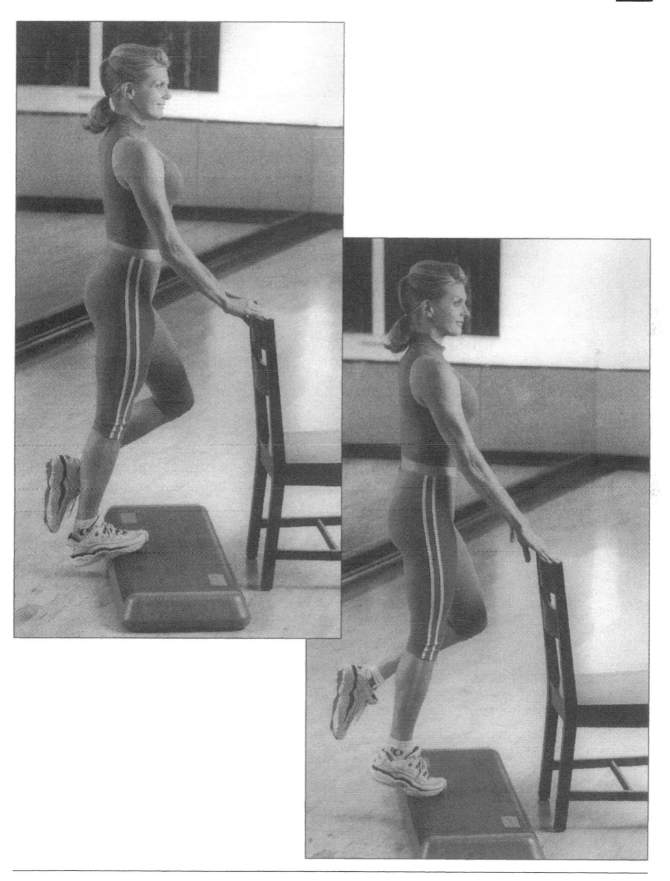

Gym Option: Leg Curl Machine
Substitute for Self-Resisted Hamstring Curl

Targets: Back of the thighs (hamstrings).

Setup: Lie face-down on the bench with your knees lined up with the axis of the machine arm and the pad resting just above your heels. Hold on to the handles below the bench. Your knees should be slightly bent in this starting position.

Move: Exhale, and bend your knees, pulling the heels toward the hips. Hold at the top of the movement, inhale, and lower your legs slowly back to the starting position.

Focus: Keep the front of your hips pressed firmly into the bench. Don't let your lower back arch or the buttocks lift as you bend your knees.

Comments: This is one of my favorite machine exercises because it is hard to target the hamstrings otherwise.

Gym Option: Inner/Outer Thigh Machine
Substitute for Side Lift with Ankle Weights (see Comments below)

Targets: Outer hip muscles (abductors) and the thighs (tensor fasciae latae).

Setup: Sit in the machine with your back against the pad. Place your feet on the rungs or against the footpads of the machine, with the leg pads against your inner thighs. Adjust the machine so that your knees are bent about 90 degrees, and the back of your thighs are parallel to the floor. Hold the handles that are under or to the sides of the seat.

Move: Exhale, and press your thighs together. Hold, inhale, and slowly open your legs to return to the starting position.

Focus: Keep a natural arch in your lower back. Don't lean forward from the waist or excessively arch as you open and close the legs.

Comments: In most gyms, this machine can be used to work the inner thighs or the outer hip muscles simply by adjusting the pads. For this reason, I've placed it in the program as an optional substitute for Side Lift with Ankle Weights, an outer hip exercise. In these photos, I'm using the machine to work my inner thighs.

Gym Option: Seated Calf Machine
Substitute for One-Legged Heel Raise

Targets: Calf muscles (gastrocnemius, soleus).

Setup: Sit up straight with the balls of your feet resting on the foot platforms and your knees under the pad. Adjust the seat so that the knees are bent about 90 degrees. Lower your heels until you feel a slight stretch in the calf muscles.

Move: Exhale and press down through the balls of your feet, lifting your heels as high as you can. Hold at the top of the movement, inhale, and return to the starting position.

Focus: Keep your weight evenly distributed across the balls of your feet. Don't roll toward the little-toe side of your foot. Try to keep your back straight throughout the exercise.

Comments: If your gym doesn't have a seated calf machine, you can substitute a standing calf machine. Strong, toned calf muscles can add shape to your lower legs and power to your stride.

Variety Option: Rear Leg Lift with Ankle Weights

Substitute for any exercise for this body part

Targets: Buttocks (gluteus) and back of the thigh (hamstring).

Setup: Stand a foot or two away from the back of a chair. Lean forward and rest your elbows on the chair. Move your right leg slightly behind your left so that your right toes are on the floor near your left heel. Your right heel is off the ground.

Move: Exhale, and slowly lift your right leg as high as you can without arching your back. Pause, inhale, and lower back down.

Focus: As you lean forward, bend from the hip—don't round your back. When you lift, your knee and toe may turn slightly to the outside. This is natural.

Variety Option: Toe Raise with Self-Resistance
Substitute for any exercise for this body part

Targets: Shin muscles (anterior tibialis).

Setup: Sit up straight on the edge of a chair with your left foot flat on the floor. Place your right heel on the top of your left foot near your toes. Place your hands on the sides of the chair seat to help keep your back straight.

Move: Exhale, and lift the front of your left foot off the floor, gently pressing down with your right foot to create resistance. Pause at the top, inhale, and lower back down.

Focus: Lift your toes as high as you can off the floor, but maintain good posture, making sure not to slump. Resist on the way up *and* on the way down, pushing gently with your right foot.

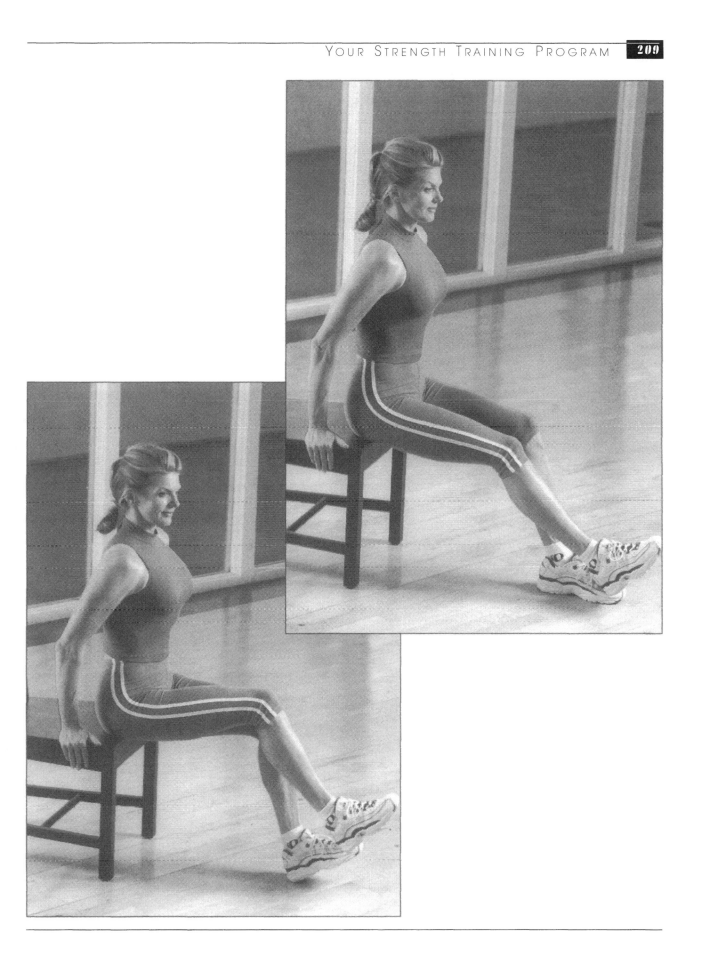

Stabilizer Exercises

Pendulum

Targets: Inner and outer thigh muscles with hips functioning as stabilizers.

Setup: Stand up tall with perfect posture. Lift your right leg out to the side until you feel your outer hip muscles working. Counterbalance this leg lift by raising both arms to the left, about shoulder height.

Move: Slowly sweep your right leg in front of your left leg and across your body until you feel your inner thigh muscles contracting. Simultaneously, sweep your arms down and across your body in the opposite direction. Repeat this side-to-side leg sweep or pendulum motion.

Focus: Try not to touch down with the moving leg. Make sure your arms are always counterbalancing the leg position. Breathe deeply throughout this exercise.

Comments: This is a good exercise to challenge your balance, and to build functional strength in your supporting leg. As you balance on one leg, the muscles in the hips, thighs, lower leg, ankles, and feet will contract isometrically.

Face-Down Plank

Targets: Shoulders, abs, hips, and legs as stabilizers.

Setup: Kneel on all fours with your hands and knees spread evenly and your neck in line with your spine. Lower your elbows to the floor and clasp your hands in front of you.

Move: Straighten your legs one at a time behind you, until you are balancing on your forearms and your toes. Pull your abs in tightly and hold your body in a straight line (as if you were a plank!). Breathe deeply, and hold this position for 10 to 30 seconds. If it is too difficult to hold the plank for more than a few seconds at first, simply bend your knees until they touch the floor.

Focus: Keep your body in a straight line. Don't let your head drop or your lower back sag. Keep breathing as you hold the plank position.

Comments: The plank is a good exercise to get your whole body working together as a dynamic unit. If one part of your body feels weak or lazy, concentrate on tightening those muscles extra hard.

Isometric Inner Thigh Squeeze

Targets: Inner thigh muscles.

Setup: Lie on your back with your knees lined up directly over your hips. Your heels should be about knee height or slightly higher. Place a firm pillow between your knees, then rest your hands on the floor beside you, palms facing down.

Move: Squeeze the pillow tightly between your knees. Breathe deeply and hold the squeeze for 5 to 10 seconds. Release slightly, but keep the pillow between your knees. Repeat the squeeze 4 to 5 times with a short rest between each one.

Focus: Keep your abs tight and your knees aligned over your hips. If it's hard to hold your legs up at first, do the squeeze with your feet resting flat on the floor.

Comments: As I'm holding the squeeze I like to think about tightening my inner thigh muscles a little more with each exhale. Try to hold the squeeze for about 4 to 5 long breaths.

Face-up Plank

Targets: Shoulders, lower back, hips, and legs as stabilizers.

Setup: Begin seated on the floor with your legs extended in front of you. Walk your hands back, bending your elbows until you can rest them. Your elbows should be directly under your shoulders, and your palms flat on the floor.

Move: Keeping your chest lifted slightly, squeeze your hips up and off the floor. You should be balanced on your heels and forearms. Breathe deeply and hold this plank position for 10 to 30 seconds. If it is too difficult to hold this plank for more than a few seconds, keep your hips on the floor and just press a little weight up until you feel your muscles contracting.

Focus: Do not lift any higher than you comfortably can. Squeeze your shoulder blades together as you hold the position. This will keep your upper body aligned and stable. Keep your neck in line with the rest of your spine at all times. Try not to let the head drop excessively forward or back.

Comments: Be patient with yourself as you build up to longer holds in this position. It may take a few weeks to get strong enough to maintain the plank position.

Push-up Position with Leg Lift

Targets: Chest, shoulders, abs, hips and legs as stabilizers.

Setup: Kneel on all fours with your hands placed about shoulder width apart. Walk your feet back until you are in either a full push-up position with your toes on the floor, or a modified push-up position with your knees bent on the floor.

Move: Balancing on either your hands and toes or hands and knees, lift one leg slightly off the floor. Breathing deeply, hold this position for about 10 seconds. Lower to both knees to rest, then change sides.

Focus: Keep your neck straight and your abs pulled in tight. Don't let your lower back sag.

Comments: Stabilizing exercises like this are a challenge, because they require you to use almost every muscle in your body. Take it slowly, and you'll see progress.

Using modified
push-up position.

One-Leg Lift

Targets: Hips, thighs, and lower legs as stabilizers.

Setup: Stand up straight with your feet together and arms hanging at your sides. Bend your knees slightly and lift one leg a few inches off the floor.

Move: Inhale, and slowly straighten your supporting leg. Hold and balance. Repeat this press up and down a few times, then change sides. Your body should rise and fall by 2 to 3 inches as you bend and straighten the supporting leg.

Focus: Each repetition should take about 10 seconds. Keep your abs pulled in and your shoulders level as you lift and lower.

Comments: Balance is an aspect of fitness that you may not have worked before. If you need more of a challenge, try this exercise with your eyes closed—it's harder than you think! Enjoy the opportunity to stretch your limits.

How to Use the Training Log

The 12-week program is divided into three 4-week blocks. Each block involves a core routine of 10 exercises covering all the major body parts. When beginning a new block, read through the exercise descriptions for those 10 exercises and practice them until you feel comfortable with them.

Gym Options

If you have access to a gym or health club, feel free to substitute one or more of the Gym Options for the exercises in the core routine aimed at the same body part. Write in your substitutions on the daily log sheets—simply cross out the prescribed exercise name and enter the name of the option you're replacing it with.

Variety Options

Variety Options are listed in Weeks Three and Four of each block. They're there to add an extra measure of fun and challenge, by lending diversity to your routine. As with the Gym Options, substitute them for the exercises in the core routine aimed at the same body part. Again, make a note of your substitutions on the daily log sheets.

Recording Your Progress

Each time you work out, write in the amount of weight you used for each exercise and the number of reps and sets you were able to do.

How Much Weight?

Choose an amount of weight that will allow you to reach fatigue within the prescribed rep range. Notice that every 4 weeks, the rep goals decrease. Lower rep goals will mean *increasing* your weight slightly so you still reach fatigue within the shorter time span. Use progressively heavier weights as your strength improves, but only use as much as you can lift *with correct form.*

Special Note to Beginners

If you're new to weight training, *start very slow and easy:* Use very light weights and progress gradually. At first, focus on technique more than on fatiguing the muscle. Study the exercise instructions carefully and try to develop a feel for the muscle being trained in each case.

When Performing Each Exercise

- Perform reps slowly and with control, approximately 4 to 7 seconds per rep.
- Keep rest periods between sets and exercises to 45 seconds.
- Perform each rep through the greatest possible range of motion.
- Try to reach fatigue within the prescribed rep range, maintaining proper form throughout.
- Focus! Perform every rep with concentration and commitment.

Scheduling

- Do at least 2 workouts per week. Do the entire routine at one time, or split it in half and do 2 mini-workouts at different times.
- Rest 48 hours between workouts for the same body parts.

At the End of 12 Weeks

Once you've gone through all three blocks, see Chapter 6 for instructions on how to continue your training.

The Plan

Strength Training Workouts: 2–3
Sets* per Exercise: 1
Reps per Set: 18–20

Cardio Training: minimum of 3 days, 30 minutes per day
Stretching: 6 days

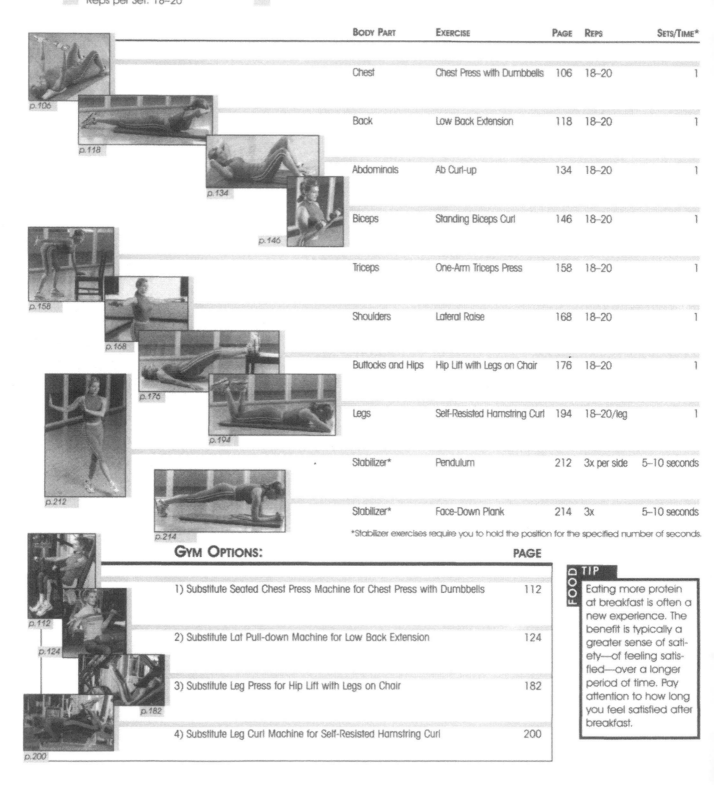

	BODY PART	EXERCISE	PAGE	REPS	SETS/TIME*
p.106	Chest	Chest Press with Dumbbells	106	18–20	1
p.118	Back	Low Back Extension	118	18–20	1
p.134	Abdominals	Ab Curl-up	134	18–20	1
p.146	Biceps	Standing Biceps Curl	146	18–20	1
p.158	Triceps	One-Arm Triceps Press	158	18–20	1
p.168	Shoulders	Lateral Raise	168	18–20	1
p.176	Buttocks and Hips	Hip Lift with Legs on Chair	176	18–20	1
p.194	Legs	Self-Resisted Hamstring Curl	194	18–20/leg	1
p.212	Stabilizer*	Pendulum	212	3x per side	5–10 seconds
p.214	Stabilizer*	Face-Down Plank	214	3x	5–10 seconds

*Stabilizer exercises require you to hold the position for the specified number of seconds.

GYM OPTIONS:

	PAGE
1) Substitute Seated Chest Press Machine for Chest Press with Dumbbells	112
2) Substitute Lat Pull-down Machine for Low Back Extension	124
3) Substitute Leg Press for Hip Lift with Legs on Chair	182
4) Substitute Leg Curl Machine for Self-Resisted Hamstring Curl	200

p.112
p.124
p.182
p.200

FOOD TIP

Eating more protein at breakfast is often a new experience. The benefit is typically a greater sense of satiety—of feeling satisfied—over a longer period of time. Pay attention to how long you feel satisfied after breakfast.

Note: Whenever an exercise option is substituted for another that targets the same body part, follow the identical reps and set recommendations.

STRENGTH TRAINING DAY 1   DATE:_____   COMMENTS:

EXERCISE	REPS	SETS	WEIGHT
Chest Press With Dumbbells			
Low Back Extension			
Ab Curl-up			
Standing Biceps Curl			
One-Arm Triceps Press			
Lateral Raise			
Hip Lift with Legs on Chair			
Self-Resisted Hamstring Curl			
Pendulum			
Face-Down Plank			

STRENGTH TRAINING DAY 2   DATE:_____   COMMENTS:

EXERCISE	REPS	SETS	WEIGHT

STRENGTH TRAINING DAY 3 (optional)   DATE:_____   COMMENTS:

EXERCISE	REPS	SETS	WEIGHT

The Plan

Strength Training Workouts: 2–3
Sets* per Exercise: 1
Reps per Set: 18–20

Cardio Training: minimum of 3 days, 30 minutes per day
Stretching: 6 days

	BODY PART	EXERCISE	PAGE	REPS	SETS/TIME*
p.106	Chest	Chest Press with Dumbbells	106	18–20	1
p.118	Back	Low Back Extension	118	18–20	1
p.134	Abdominals	Ab Curl-up	134	18–20	1
p.146	Biceps	Standing Biceps Curl	146	18–20	1
p.158	Triceps	One-Arm Triceps Press	158	18–20	1
p.168	Shoulders	Lateral Raise	168	18–20	1
p.176	Buttocks and Hips	Hip Lift with Legs on Chair	176	18–20	1
p.194	Legs	Self-Resisted Hamstring Curl	194	18–20/leg	1
p.212	Stabilizer*	Pendulum	212	3x per side	5–10 seconds
p.214	Stabilizer*	Face-Down Plank	214	3x	5–10 seconds

*Stabilizer exercises require you to hold the position for the specified number of seconds.

GYM OPTIONS:

	PAGE
1) Substitute Seated Chest Press Machine for Chest Press with Dumbbells	112
2) Substitute Lat Pull-down Machine for Low Back Extension	124
3) Substitute Leg Press for Hip Lift with Legs on Chair	182
4) Substitute Leg Curl Machine for Self-Resisted Hamstring Curl	200

p.112
p.124
p.182
p.200

FOOD TIP

Using food as a tranquilizer is all too common. Try to cultivate a wide variety of alternative soothing habits to take its place: reading a good book, flipping through your favorite magazine, playing a game, picking flowers, getting your nails done, taking a class, starting a new hobby or craft.

Note: Whenever an exercise option is substituted for another that targets the same body part, follow the identical reps and set recommendations.

STRENGTH TRAINING DAY 1   DATE:_____   COMMENTS:

EXERCISE	REPS	SETS	WEIGHT
Chest Press With Dumbbells			
Low Back Extension			
Ab Curl-up			
Standing Biceps Curl			
One-Arm Triceps Press			
Lateral Raise			
Hip Lift with Legs on Chair			
Self-Resisted Hamstring Curl			
Pendulum			
Face-Down Plank			

STRENGTH TRAINING DAY 2   DATE:_____   COMMENTS:

EXERCISE	REPS	SETS	WEIGHT

STRENGTH TRAINING DAY 3 (optional)   DATE:_____   COMMENTS:

EXERCISE	REPS	SETS	WEIGHT

The Plan

Strength Training Workouts: 2–3
Sets* per Exercise: 1
Reps per Set: 18–20

Cardio Training: minimum of 3 days, 30 minutes per day
Stretching: 6 days

	BODY PART	EXERCISE	PAGE	REPS	SETS/TIME*
p.106	Chest	Chest Press with Dumbbells	106	18–20	1
p.118	Back	Low Back Extension	118	18–20	1
p.134	Abdominals	Ab Curl-up	134	18–20	1
p.146	Biceps	Standing Biceps Curl	146	18–20	1
p.158	Triceps	One-Arm Triceps Press	158	18–20	1
p.168	Shoulders	Lateral Raise	168	18–20	1
p.176	Buttocks and Hips	Hip Lift with Legs on Chair	176	18–20	1
p.194	Legs	Self-Resisted Hamstring Curl	194	18–20/leg	1
p.212	Stabilizer*	Pendulum	212	3x per side	5–10 seconds
p.214	Stabilizer*	Face-Down Plank	214	3x	5–10 seconds

*Stabilizer exercises require you to hold the position for the specified number of seconds.

GYM OPTIONS: PAGE

p.112

p.124

p.182

p.200

	PAGE
1) Substitute Seated Chest Press Machine for Chest Press with Dumbbells	112
2) Substitute Lat Pull-down Machine for Low Back Extension	124
3) Substitute Leg Press for Hip Lift with Legs on Chair	182
4) Substitute Leg Curl Machine for Self-Resisted Hamstring Curl	200

FOOD TIP

Eating when you are hungry, stopping when you've had enough: This is the basic rule of thumb for managing your weight successfully no matter what you are eating.

Variety Options: Page
1) Back: Seated Back Flye   128
2) Abdominals: Oblique Ab Curl   140
3) Buttocks and Hips: Front Lunge   188

Note: Whenever an exercise option is substituted for another that targets the same body part, follow the identical reps and set recommendations.

STRENGTH TRAINING DAY 1   DATE:_____

COMMENTS:

EXERCISE	REPS	SETS	WEIGHT
Chest Press With Dumbbells			
Low Back Extension			
Ab Curl-up			
Standing Biceps Curl			
One-Arm Triceps Press			
Lateral Raise			
Hip Lift with Legs on Chair			
Self-Resisted Hamstring Curl			
Pendulum			
Face-Down Plank			

STRENGTH TRAINING DAY 2   DATE:_____

COMMENTS:

EXERCISE	REPS	SETS	WEIGHT

STRENGTH TRAINING DAY 3 (optional)   DATE:_____

COMMENTS:

EXERCISE	REPS	SETS	WEIGHT

BLOCK 1 *Week Four*

The Plan

Strength Training Workouts: 2–3
Sets* per Exercise: 1
Reps per Set: 18–20

Cardio Training: minimum of 3 days, 30 minutes per day
Stretching: 6 days

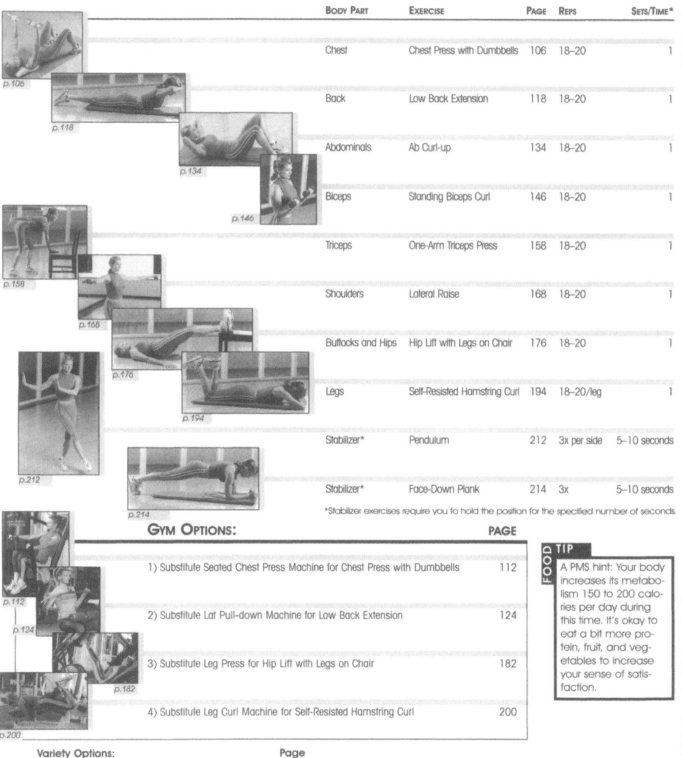

	Body Part	Exercise	Page	Reps	Sets/Time*
	Chest	Chest Press with Dumbbells	106	18–20	1
	Back	Low Back Extension	118	18–20	1
	Abdominals	Ab Curl-up	134	18–20	1
	Biceps	Standing Biceps Curl	146	18–20	1
	Triceps	One-Arm Triceps Press	158	18–20	1
	Shoulders	Lateral Raise	168	18–20	1
	Buttocks and Hips	Hip Lift with Legs on Chair	176	18–20	1
	Legs	Self-Resisted Hamstring Curl	194	18–20/leg	1
	Stabilizer*	Pendulum	212	3x per side	5–10 seconds
	Stabilizer*	Face-Down Plank	214	3x	5–10 seconds

*Stabilizer exercises require you to hold the position for the specified number of seconds.

GYM OPTIONS: PAGE

1) Substitute Seated Chest Press Machine for Chest Press with Dumbbells   112

2) Substitute Lat Pull-down Machine for Low Back Extension   124

3) Substitute Leg Press for Hip Lift with Legs on Chair   182

4) Substitute Leg Curl Machine for Self-Resisted Hamstring Curl   200

FOOD TIP

A PMS hint: Your body increases its metabolism 150 to 200 calories per day during this time. It's okay to eat a bit more protein, fruit, and vegetables to increase your sense of satisfaction.

Variety Options: Page
1) Back: Seated Back Flye   128
2) Abdominals: Oblique Ab Curl   140
3) Buttocks and Hips: Front Lunge   188

Note: Whenever an exercise option is substituted for another that targets the same body part, follow the identical reps and set recommendations.

STRENGTH TRAINING DAY 1   DATE:_____   COMMENTS:

EXERCISE	REPS	SETS	WEIGHT
Chest Press With Dumbbells			
Low Back Extension			
Ab Curl-up			
Standing Biceps Curl			
One-Arm Triceps Press			
Lateral Raise			
Hip Lift with Legs on Chair			
Self-Resisted Hamstring Curl			
Pendulum			
Face-Down Plank			

STRENGTH TRAINING DAY 2   DATE:_____   COMMENTS:

EXERCISE	REPS	SETS	WEIGHT

STRENGTH TRAINING DAY 3 (optional)   DATE:_____   COMMENTS:

EXERCISE	REPS	SETS	WEIGHT

The Plan

Strength Training Workouts: 2–3
Sets* per Exercise: 1–2
Reps per Set: 15

Cardio Training: minimum of 3 days, 30 minutes per day
Stretching: 6 days

	Body Part	Exercise	Page	Reps	Sets/Time*
	Chest	Push-up	108	15	1–2
	Back	One-Arm Row with Dumbbells	120	15	1–2
	Abdominals	Combo Ab Curl	136	15	1–2
	Biceps	Biceps Curl with Reverse Grip	148	15	1–2
	Triceps	One-Arm French Press	160	15	1–2
	Shoulders	Overhead Press	170	15	1–2
	Buttocks and Hips	Squat Holding Dumbbells	178	15	1–2
	Legs	Side Lift with Ankle Weights	196	15/leg	1–2
	Stabilizer*	Isometric Inner Thigh Squeeze	216	3x per side	5–10 seconds
	Stabilizer*	Face-up Plank	218	3x	5–10 seconds

p.108, p.120, p136, p.148, p.160, p.170, p.178, p.196, p.216, p.218

*Stabilizer exercises require you to hold the position for the specified number of seconds.

Gym Options:

	PAGE
1) Substitute Straight Bar Bench Press for Push-up	114
2) Substitute Cable Curl for Biceps Curl with Reverse Grip	152
3) Substitute Leg Extension Machine for Squat Holding Dumbbells	184
4) Substitute Inner/Outer Thigh Machine for Side Lift with Ankle Weights	202

p.114, p.152, p.184, p.202

FOOD TIP

Even when trying to lose fat weight, most people need at least 80 to 120 calories per waking hour. If you eat 400 calories in a meal, expect to be ready to eat again in 3 to 5 hours.

Note: Whenever an exercise option is substituted for another that targets the same body part, follow the identical reps and set recommendations.

Strength Training Day 1   DATE:_____   COMMENTS:

EXERCISE	REPS	SETS	WEIGHT
Push-up			
One-Arm Row with Dumbbells			
Combo Ab Curl			
Biceps Curl with Reverse Grip			
One-Arm French Press			
Overhead Press			
Squat Holding Dumbbells			
Side Lift with Ankle Weights			
Isometric Inner Thigh Squeeze			
Face-up Plank			

Strength Training Day 2   DATE:_____   COMMENTS:

EXERCISE	REPS	SETS	WEIGHT

Strength Training Day 3 (optional)   DATE:_____   COMMENTS:

EXERCISE	REPS	SETS	WEIGHT

The Plan

Strength Training Workouts: 2–3
Sets* per Exercise: 1–2
Reps per Set: 15

Cardio Training: minimum of 3 days, 30 minutes per day
Stretching: 6 days

BODY PART	EXERCISE	PAGE	REPS	SETS/TIME*
Chest	Push-up	108	15	1–2
Back	One-Arm Row with Dumbbells	120	15	1–2
Abdominals	Combo Ab Curl	136	15	1–2
Biceps	Biceps Curl with Reverse Grip	148	15	1–2
Triceps	One-Arm French Press	160	15	1–2
Shoulders	Overhead Press	170	15	1–2
Buttocks and Hips	Squat Holding Dumbbells	178	15	1–2
Legs	Side Lift with Ankle Weights	196	15/leg	1–2
Stabilizer*	Isometric Inner Thigh Squeeze	216	3x per side	5–10 seconds
Stabilizer*	Face-up Plank	218	3x	5–10 seconds

*Stabilizer exercises require you to hold the position for the specified number of seconds.

GYM OPTIONS:	PAGE
1) Substitute Straight Bar Bench Press for Push-up	114
2) Substitute Cable Curl for Biceps Curl with Reverse Grip	152
3) Substitute Leg Extension Machine for Squat Holding Dumbbells	184
4) Substitute Inner/Outer Thigh Machine for Side Lift with Ankle Weights	202

FOOD TIP

You may notice that certain carbohydrates affect you differently than others. Some people find that eating bread makes them feel bloated and uncomfortable. Others notice those sensations with pasta, and still others with fruit juices. Pay attention and see if there are any specific carbohydrates you don't handle well.

Note: Whenever an exercise option is substituted for another that targets the same body part, follow the identical reps and set recommendations.

STRENGTH TRAINING DAY 1 DATE:_____

EXERCISE	REPS	SETS	WEIGHT
Push-up			
One-Arm Row with Dumbbells			
Combo Ab Curl			
Biceps Curl with Reverse Grip			
One-Arm French Press			
Overhead Press			
Squat Holding Dumbbells			
Side Lift with Ankle Weights			
Isometric Inner Thigh Squeeze			
Face-up Plank			

COMMENTS:

STRENGTH TRAINING DAY 2 DATE:_____

EXERCISE	REPS	SETS	WEIGHT

COMMENTS:

STRENGTH TRAINING DAY 3 (optional) DATE:_____

EXERCISE	REPS	SETS	WEIGHT

COMMENTS:

The Plan

Strength Training Workouts: 2–3
Sets* per Exercise: 1–2
Reps per Set: 15

Cardio Training: minimum of 3 days, 30 minutes per day
Stretching: 6 days

Body Part	Exercise	Page	Reps	Sets/Time*
Chest	Push-up	108	15	1–2
Back	One-Arm Row with Dumbbells	120	15	1–2
Abdominals	Combo Ab Curl	136	15	1–2
Biceps	Biceps Curl with Reverse Grip	148	15	1–2
Triceps	One-Arm French Press	160	15	1–2
Shoulders	Overhead Press	170	15	1–2
Buttocks and Hips	Squat Holding Dumbbells	178	15	1–2
Legs	Side Lift with Ankle Weights	196	15/leg	1–2
Stabilizer*	Isometric Inner Thigh Squeeze	216	3x per side	5–10 seconds
Stabilizer*	Face-up Plank	218	3x	5–10 seconds

*Stabilizer exercises require you to hold the position for the specified number of seconds.

GYM OPTIONS:	PAGE
1) Substitute Straight Bar Bench Press for Push-up	114
2) Substitute Cable Curl for Biceps Curl with Reverse Grip	152
3) Substitute Leg Extension Machine for Squat Holding Dumbbells	184
4) Substitute Inner/Outer Thigh Machine for Side Lift with Ankle Weights	202

Variety Options:	Page
1) Abdominals: Reverse Ab Curl	142
2) Buttocks and Hips: Wall Squat with One-Leg Lift	190
3) Legs: Rear Leg Lift with Ankle Weights	206

FOOD TIP

Most of us enjoy sweets—we're literally born that way. So it's important to learn how to eat a sweet treat. The best time is right after a meal. First, you are less hungry and will be satisfied with less. Second, the protein in the meal will protect you from a blood sugar roller coaster that too often leads to craving—and consuming—more and more sugar.

Note: Whenever an exercise option is substituted for another that targets the same body part, follow the identical reps and set recommendations.

STRENGTH TRAINING DAY 1   DATE:_____

COMMENTS:

EXERCISE	REPS	SETS	WEIGHT
Push-up			
One-Arm Row with Dumbbells			
Combo Ab Curl			
Biceps Curl with Reverse Grip			
One-Arm French Press			
Overhead Press			
Squat Holding Dumbbells			
Side Lift with Ankle Weights			
Isometric Inner Thigh Squeeze			
Face-up Plank			

STRENGTH TRAINING DAY 2   DATE:_____

COMMENTS:

EXERCISE	REPS	SETS	WEIGHT

STRENGTH TRAINING DAY 3 (optional)   DATE:_____

COMMENTS:

EXERCISE	REPS	SETS	WEIGHT

The Plan

▪ Strength Training Workouts: 2–3	▪ Cardio Training: minimum of 3 days, 30 minutes per day
▪ Sets* per Exercise: 1–2	▪ Stretching: 6 days
▪ Reps per Set: 15	

BODY PART	EXERCISE	PAGE	REPS	SETS/TIME*
Chest	Push-up	108	15	1–2
Back	One-Arm Row with Dumbbells	120	15	1–2
Abdominals	Combo Ab Curl	136	15	1–2
Biceps	Biceps Curl with Reverse Grip	148	15	1–2
Triceps	One-Arm French Press	160	15	1–2
Shoulders	Overhead Press	170	15	1–2
Buttocks and Hips	Squat Holding Dumbbells	178	15	1–2
Legs	Side Lift with Ankle Weights	196	15/leg	1–2
Stabilizer*	Isometric Inner Thigh Squeeze	216	3x per side	5–10 seconds
Stabilizer*	Face-up Plank	218	3x	5–10 seconds

*Stabilizer exercises require you to hold the position for the specified number of seconds.

p.108
p.120
p136
p.148
p.160
p.170
p.178
p.196
p.216
p.218

GYM OPTIONS:	PAGE
1) Substitute Straight Bar Bench Press for Push-up	114
2) Substitute Cable Curl for Biceps Curl with Reverse Grip	152
3) Substitute Leg Extension Machine for Squat Holding Dumbbells	184
4) Substitute Inner/Outer Thigh Machine for Side Lift with Ankle Weights	202

p.114
p.152
p.184
p.202

FOOD TIP

How do you feel throughout the day after eating a better balance of carbohydrates, protein, and fat? Many people notice they have better energy and more stamina all day long. They don't need to grab for the candy jar or a cup of coffee to get through the afternoon.

Variety Options: | **Page**
1) Abdominals: Reverse Ab Curl | 142
2) Buttocks and Hips: Wall Squat with One-Leg Lift | 190
3) Legs: Rear Leg Lift with Ankle Weights | 206

Note: Whenever an exercise option is substituted for another that targets the same body part, follow the identical reps and set recommendations.

STRENGTH TRAINING DAY 1 DATE:_____

COMMENTS:

EXERCISE	REPS	SETS	WEIGHT
Push-up			
One-Arm Row with Dumbbells			
Combo Ab Curl			
Biceps Curl with Reverse Grip			
One-Arm French Press			
Overhead Press			
Squat Holding Dumbbells			
Side Lift with Ankle Weights			
Isometric Inner Thigh Squeeze			
Face-up Plank			

STRENGTH TRAINING DAY 2 DATE:_____

COMMENTS:

EXERCISE	REPS	SETS	WEIGHT

STRENGTH TRAINING DAY 3 (optional) DATE:_____

COMMENTS:

EXERCISE	REPS	SETS	WEIGHT

The Plan

Strength Training Workouts: 2–3
Sets* per Exercise: 1–2
Reps per Set: 10–12

Cardio Training: minimum of 3 days, 30 minutes per day
Stretching: 6 days

BODY PART	EXERCISE	PAGE	REPS	SETS/TIME*
Chest	Chest Flye	110	10–12	1–2
Back	High Elbow Row	122	10–12	1–2
Abdominals	Assisted Ab Curl-up	138	10–12	1–2
Biceps	Preacher Curl	150	10–12	1–2
Triceps	Triceps Dip on Chair	162	10–12	1–2
Shoulders	Rear Raise	172	10–12	1–2
Buttocks and Hips	Skier's Lunge	180	10–12	1–2
Legs	One-Legged Heel Raise	198	10–12/leg	1–2
Stabilizer*	Push-up Position with Leg Lift	220	3x per side	5–10 seconds
Stabilizer*	One-Leg Lift	222	3x	5–10 seconds

*Stabilizer exercises require you to hold the position for the specified number of seconds.

GYM OPTIONS:	PAGE
1) Substitute Cable Low Row for High Elbow Row	126
2) Substitute Cable Triceps Pull-down for Triceps Dip on Chair	164
3) Substitute Smith Rack Lunge for Skier's Lunge	186
4) Substitute Seated (or Standing) Calf Machine for One-Legged Heel Raise	204

FOOD TIP

Women shouldn't despair when they feel hungrier and less content just before their period. Progesterone rises during this time and affects how your body metabolizes carbohydrates. Despite craving sugar and carbohydrates, though, you may actually feel more content by eating more protein. Try it and see.

Note: Whenever an exercise option is substituted for another that targets the same body part, follow the identical reps and set recommendations.

STRENGTH TRAINING DAY 1   DATE:_____

COMMENTS:

EXERCISE	REPS	SETS	WEIGHT
Chest Flye			
High Elbow Row			
Assisted Ab Curl-up			
Preacher Curl			
Triceps Dip on Chair			
Rear Raise			
Skier's Lunge			
One-Legged Heel Raise			
Push-up Position with Leg Lift			
One-Leg Lift			

STRENGTH TRAINING DAY 2   DATE:_____

COMMENTS:

EXERCISE	REPS	SETS	WEIGHT

STRENGTH TRAINING DAY 3 (optional)   DATE:_____

COMMENTS:

EXERCISE	REPS	SETS	WEIGHT

The Plan

Strength Training Workouts: 2–3
Sets* per Exercise: 1–2
Reps per Set: 10–12

Cardio Training: minimum of 3 days, 30 minutes per day
Stretching: 6 days

Body Part	Exercise	Page	Reps	Sets/Time*
Chest	Chest Flye	110	10–12	1–2
Back	High Elbow Row	122	10–12	1–2
Abdominals	Assisted Ab Curl-up	138	10–12	1–2
Biceps	Preacher Curl	150	10–12	1–2
Triceps	Triceps Dip on Chair	162	10–12	1–2
Shoulders	Rear Raise	172	10–12	1–2
Buttocks and Hips	Skier's Lunge	180	10–12	1–2
Legs	One-Legged Heel Raise	198	10–12/leg	1–2
Stabilizer*	Push-up Position with Leg Lift	220	3x per side	5–10 seconds
Stabilizer*	One-Leg Lift	222	3x	5–10 seconds

*Stabilizer exercises require you to hold the position for the specified number of seconds.

Gym Options:	Page
1) Substitute Cable Low Row for High Elbow Row	126
2) Substitute Cable Triceps Pull-down for Triceps Dip on Chair	164
3) Substitute Smith Rack Lunge for Skier's Lunge	186
4) Substitute Seated (or Standing) Calf Machine for One-Legged Heel Raise	204

FOOD TIP

Too often when people discover how much better they feel with more protein and fat in their food, they start to think carbohydrates are bad. Nothing could be further from the truth. We need plenty of carbohydrates to fuel our brains and our muscles. The key is balance.

Note: Whenever an exercise option is substituted for another that targets the same body part, follow the identical reps and set recommendations.

STRENGTH TRAINING DAY 1   DATE:_____   COMMENTS:

EXERCISE	REPS	SETS	WEIGHT
Chest Flye			
High Elbow Row			
Assisted Ab Curl-up			
Preacher Curl			
Triceps Dip on Chair			
Rear Raise			
Skier's Lunge			
One-Legged Heel Raise			
Push-up Position with Leg Lift			
One-Leg Lift			

STRENGTH TRAINING DAY 2   DATE:_____   COMMENTS:

EXERCISE	REPS	SETS	WEIGHT

STRENGTH TRAINING DAY 3 (optional)   DATE:_____   COMMENTS:

EXERCISE	REPS	SETS	WEIGHT

The Plan

▪ Strength Training Workouts: 2–3
▪ Sets* per Exercise: 1–2
▪ Reps per Set: 10–12

▪ Cardio Training: minimum of 3 days, 30 minutes per day
▪ Stretching: 6 days

BODY PART	EXERCISE	PAGE	REPS	SETS/TIME*
Chest	Chest Flye	110	10–12	1–2
Back	High Elbow Row	122	10–12	1–2
Abdominals	Assisted Ab Curl-up	138	10–12	1–2
Biceps	Preacher Curl	150	10–12	1–2
Triceps	Triceps Dip on Chair	162	10–12	1–2
Shoulders	Rear Raise	172	10–12	1–2
Buttocks and Hips	Skier's Lunge	180	10–12	1–2
Legs	One-Legged Heel Raise	198	10–12/leg	1–2
Stabilizer*	Push-up Position with Leg Lift	220	3x per side	5–10 seconds
Stabilizer*	One-Leg Lift	222	3x	5–10 seconds

*Stabilizer exercises require you to hold the position for the specified number of seconds.

p.110 · p.122 · p.138 · p.150 · p.162 · p.172 · p.180 · p.198 · p.220 · p.222

GYM OPTIONS:

	PAGE
1) Substitute Cable Low Row for High Elbow Row	126
2) Substitute Cable Triceps Pull-down for Triceps Dip on Chair	164
3) Substitute Smith Rack Lunge for Skier's Lunge	186
4) Substitute Seated (or Standing) Calf Machine for One-Legged Heel Raise	204

p.126 · p.164 · p.186 · p.204

FOOD TIP

Do you struggle with nighttime snacking? Eating more protein and adequate calories through the day can really quiet the desire for nighttime snacks. Even if you decide you want a snack, it is often satisfied with something very modest.

Variety Options:

	Page
1) Back: Back Extension with Rotation	130
2) Biceps: Concentration Curl	154
3) Legs: Toe Raise with Self-Resistance	208

Note: Whenever an exercise option is substituted for another that targets the same body part, follow the identical reps and set recommendations.

STRENGTH TRAINING DAY 1　　DATE:_____

EXERCISE	REPS	SETS	WEIGHT
Chest Flye			
High Elbow Row			
Assisted Ab Curl-up			
Preacher Curl			
Triceps Dip on Chair			
Rear Raise			
Skier's Lunge			
One-Legged Heel Raise			
Push-up Position with Leg Lift			
One-Leg Lift			

COMMENTS:

STRENGTH TRAINING DAY 2　　DATE:_____

EXERCISE	REPS	SETS	WEIGHT

COMMENTS:

STRENGTH TRAINING DAY 3 (optional)　DATE:_____

EXERCISE	REPS	SETS	WEIGHT

COMMENTS:

The Plan

Strength Training Workouts: 2–3
Sets* per Exercise: 1–2
Reps per Set: 10–12

Cardio Training: minimum of 3 days, 30 minutes per day
Stretching: 6 days

	BODY PART	EXERCISE	PAGE	REPS	SETS/TIME*
	Chest	Chest Flye	110	10–12	1–2
	Back	High Elbow Row	122	10–12	1–2
	Abdominals	Assisted Ab Curl-up	138	10–12	1–2
	Biceps	Preacher Curl	150	10–12	1–2
	Triceps	Triceps Dip on Chair	162	10–12	1–2
	Shoulders	Rear Raise	172	10–12	1–2
	Buttocks and Hips	Skier's Lunge	180	10–12	1–2
	Legs	One-Legged Heel Raise	198	10–12/leg	1–2
	Stabilizer*	Push-up Position with Leg Lift	220	3x per side	5–10 seconds
	Stabilizer*	One-Leg Lift	222	3x	5–10 seconds

p.110 *p.122* *p.138* *p.150* *p.162* *p.172* *p.180* *p.198* *p.220* *p.222*

*Stabilizer exercises require you to hold the position for the specified number of seconds.

GYM OPTIONS:

	PAGE
1) Substitute Cable Low Row for High Elbow Row	126
2) Substitute Cable Triceps Pull-down for Triceps Dip on Chair	164
3) Substitute Smith Rack Lunge for Skier's Lunge	186
4) Substitute Seated (or Standing) Calf Machine for One-Legged Heel Raise	204

p.126 *p.164* *p.186* *p.204*

FOOD TIP
Snacking has become an institution in our culture, and it isn't all bad. If your meals are spread far apart, a snack can be a great way to keep your energy level up and keep you from getting overhungry—and overeating!

Variety Options:

	Page
1) Back: Back Extension with Rotation	130
2) Biceps: Concentration Curl	154
3) Legs: Toe Raise with Self-Resistance	208

Note: Whenever an exercise option is substituted for another that targets the same body part, follow the identical reps and set recommendations.

STRENGTH TRAINING DAY 1   DATE:_____   COMMENTS:

EXERCISE	REPS	SETS	WEIGHT
Chest Flye			
High Elbow Row			
Assisted Ab Curl-up			
Preacher Curl			
Triceps Dip on Chair			
Rear Raise			
Skier's Lunge			
One-Legged Heel Raise			
Push-up Position with Leg Lift			
One-Leg Lift			

STRENGTH TRAINING DAY 2   DATE:_____   COMMENTS:

EXERCISE	REPS	SETS	WEIGHT

STRENGTH TRAINING DAY 3 (optional) DATE:_____   COMMENTS:

EXERCISE	REPS	SETS	WEIGHT

Chapter 11

Fuel Up and
Slim Down

Naturally, what you put into your body has a big impact on your weight—not to mention your general health and energy level. If you want to get the most out of your strength training, it's important to supplement your efforts with sensible nutrition. The trouble is, the subject of nutrition can be so terribly confusing. There are so many weight loss theories that trying to separate truth from fiction can be an overwhelming task. In this chapter, I'll try to make it a little easier by giving you a simple formula for healthy eating.

The Road to Independence

People often tell me their reason for starting a new program is that they're feeling a lack of control over their eating. Feeling this way, they're likely to subject themselves to a highly restrictive diet—one that's much too rigid to stick with. In a few weeks, they've fallen off the diet, gained back all the weight they'd lost, and they feel like they've failed. In reality, though, the diet failed *them*.

The fact is, diets don't work. Dieting creates a sense of deprivation that almost guarantees failure. Worse yet, extreme calorie cutting can lower your metabolism, making you more likely to gain weight when you finally—inevitably—go off the diet. The better solution is to develop a new set of eating habits altogether—a new way of thinking about eating that isn't so restrictive. A set of eating habits *flexible* enough to comfortably sustain you, year in and year out.

The goal of this chapter is to help you become an *independent eater*—one who can make sensible eating choices on your own. Becoming an independent eater involves an ongoing process of assessing your needs and adjusting your food choices accordingly. It means evolving from rigid eating patterns or being told what to eat, to understanding the implications of food choices and making them in accordance with the ups and downs of your lifestyle. Independent eating means that you:

- Eat when you're hungry and stop when you feel satisfied.
- Enjoy the foods you truly love to eat.
- Choose foods that enhance your physiological well-being.
- Know that the next time you get hungry, you'll have the opportunity to nourish and nurture yourself again.

To accomplish this, I've developed a formula I call my 1-2-3 Plan. It's not a diet, but a framework within which you can make eating choices that suit your own tastes and goals. I've tried to create a plan that has just enough structure to give you a sense of things being under control again, without being overly restrictive.

The 1-2-3 Plan

The tools that make this plan work are:

The Nutritional Information in This Chapter

The information in this chapter will give you the background you need to take charge of your own nutritional needs.

The 1-2-3 Food Table

This table will show you how to maintain the specified balance of recommended nutrients.

Your Nutritional Journal

The Nutritional Journal at the end of this chapter will help you monitor your hunger level to determine the optimal caloric intake for your energy needs.

The Nutrients

Protein, Carbohydrate, Fat

You've heard these terms before, I'm sure! These are the nutrients your body uses for fuel. And I'm sure you've heard the term "balanced diet" as well. The balance of nutrients in your diet has a powerful impact on how long you feel satisfied after eating, and on your ability to lose weight.

I've tried many different eating plans—from high-protein diets, to others in which meals consist almost entirely of carbohydrates. I've found that, for me, a more evenly balanced plan works best. The recommendations in this chapter are based on a caloric distribution of:

- 25 percent protein
- 50 percent carbohydrate
- 25 percent fat

Maintaining this ratio of protein, carbohydrate, and fat in each meal will help keep your overall calorie intake down without depriving yourself of much of the pleasure of eating. You can still eat many of your favorite foods within the framework. And, because it's not extremely high or low in any one type of food, it makes it easy to get all the necessary nutrients.

Two Types of Carbohydrates

The amount of carbohydrate in your diet can make the difference between gaining and losing weight. Carbohydrate is essential, and most of your calories during the day will come from this nutrient. However, carbohydrates include a variety of foods—everything from doughnuts to broccoli! In order to keep our caloric intake under control, we're going to make an important distinction between two classes of carbohydrates: **fruits and vegetables** and **starches.** We'll be balancing small quantities of starchy carbohydrates with greater quantities of low-calorie fruits and vegetables.

Americans have been conditioned over the years to eat larger and larger quantities of starches. Pastas, breads, bagels, cereals, and muffins are often the dieter's staple foods. The trouble is, they can be high in empty calories. My 1-2-3 Plan is for anyone who wants to lose weight. But it's particularly effective for those people who have gained weight

> *"I've been chubby all my life and tried to lose weight in college through dieting. I might have lost some weight, but I didn't feel healthy and fit. Now I don't starve myself anymore and I eat anything I like in moderation without guilt because I work out."*
>
> **Aimee, age 29**

by eating too many starchy carbohydrates, and now find it exceedingly difficult to lose it.

Following this plan, you'll still enjoy a wide variety of carbohydrates, but in more modest amounts than you're probably used to. Specifically, it's the starchy carbohydrates we'll be cutting back on. You'll still get plenty of carbohydrates in the form of fruits and vegetables. This, plus maintaining the proper balance of the other nutrients, will enable all the carbohydrates in your diet to be more effectively burned as fuel.

Protein

Protein may make up a larger portion of the meals on this plan than you're used to. On and off over the years, Americans have been scolded for eating too much protein. Yet there's plenty of evidence now to suggest that many people don't eat enough of this important nutrient. Protein is essential for building lean muscle tissue. My plan offers you protein from many different sources, including meats, legumes, and soy-based protein (tofu, for example).

Fat

You may be surprised at the amount of fat in each meal. In recent years, weight-conscious Americans have become obsessed with eliminating fat from their diets. But fat serves an essential function: Along with protein, fat helps us feel satisfied after a meal. On my program, you don't have to worry about every little gram of fat you put into your mouth; you simply need to be responsible and limit your consumption of it to 25 percent of your total calories.

More significant than the total amount of fat in your diet are excessive amounts of **saturated fats.** Saturated fats are those that are solid at room temperature—most dairy products, for instance, contain mostly saturated fat. Unsaturated fats are found in vegetable oils, nuts, seeds, and other plant foods like avocados and olives. Whenever possible, it's best to choose unsaturated over saturated fats.

Most animal-based proteins have a reasonable mix of unsaturated and saturated fats, so on this program you'll be free to choose lean cuts of beef, poultry (chicken and turkey), fish, pork, or lamb to enjoy on a regular basis.

The Basics

Almost all the foods we eat contain a mixture of protein, carbohydrate, and fat. For the purposes of this program, I'll categorize foods according to the most significant nutrient they contain.

You may be wondering: How can I possibly keep track of protein, carbohydrate, and fat at every meal? That's easy—you simply follow my 1-2-3 Plan. Here are the elements of the plan:

- Finding a calorie intake that will support fat loss without creating a sense of deprivation;
- Eating throughout the day to limit cravings and keep energy up;
- Becoming tuned in to feelings of hunger and satisfaction;
- Choosing the proper balance of nutrients;
- Building in enough flexibility so that you can still enjoy the foods you want within the framework.

Let's explore these points one by one.

Calories?
Your Body Knows Best

How many calories should you be eating? Unfortunately, there's no easy answer. Everyone knows that eating more than we need leads to storing fat. But ironically, eating too few calories can actually make it even harder to lose fat and maintain a lower weight.

My program is based on an intake of approximately 1,500 calories a day. This is a reasonable number to support fat loss in an active person. However, everyone's metabolism is different, so consider that 1,500 number as a starting point. In addition, caloric needs can change, depending on how much exercise you're doing. The best indicator of your exact caloric needs is your hunger level. Only your body can tell you how many calories you need in order to feel satisfied.

Here are three strategies to try if you're not feeling satisfied with your starting caloric level:

1. Eat more! If you're not feeling satisfied with the planned calorie level after the first few days, it's perfectly acceptable to slightly adjust your portions and caloric intake until you feel satisfied. (Key word: *slightly*.)

Remember, for this program to become part of a long-term healthy lifestyle, you need to listen to your body and find the calorie level that will keep you from being hungry all day.

2. Eat more protein and vegetables or fruits until you honestly feel satisfied.

3. Eat slowly enough that your body has time to register that you've eaten. Slow down and really taste your food—enjoying the taste of food is an important part of the satisfaction of eating.

There's one important rule when adjusting your calorie intake in response to your body's needs: that's to *be honest with yourself*. Listen to your hunger, not your habits, when deciding how much to eat.

Eating Throughout the Day

It's a fact that whenever we're overly hungry, we're more likely to overeat or binge. Too often, we get busy at work or with errands and we skip meals—deferring those calories until the inevitable snacking at night. This is not the way to lose fat weight or maintain a lean, fit body. It's better to eat throughout the day and not let yourself get ravenous. Enjoy each meal and you'll feel energetic and positive all day long.

On this program, you'll be eating four balanced meals per day. By evenly spacing these meals, you'll have the fuel you need for energy during your waking hours. Plan to eat your first meal within two hours after rising in the morning. After that, eat another meal every 3 to 4 hours. A typical day might look like this:

> I can't emphasize enough how important your first foods of the day are in the big picture of managing your weight. Whatever you do, don't skip breakfast! A good first meal is crucial to getting your metabolism revved up and stabilizing your energy level for the day. This is why I recommend eating breakfast within two hours after waking.

Meal #1: 8:00 A.M.
Meal #2: 12:00 noon
Meal #3: 3:30 P.M.
Meal #4: 7:00 P.M.

If your day is particularly hectic and you only have time for a snack instead of one of your scheduled meals, try to avoid filling up on foods that are all starch or sugar, such as a bagel, a candy bar, or a bag of pretzels. Reach instead for a more balanced snack—some fruit and cheese, a peanut butter and jelly sandwich, or yogurt and nuts.

The Role of Hunger and Satisfaction

Remember, it's perfectly acceptable to adjust your overall calorie intake until you feel satisfied. This gives you the kind of control most of us need to successfully lose weight. If you're eating the prescribed meals at the prescribed meal times and finding yourself truly hungry between meals, eat something! Your body is telling you that you need more fuel. If it's only an hour until your next meal, have a piece of fruit or vegetable. If you have three or more hours until your next meal, try a heartier snack.

On my 1-2-3 Plan protein and fat are two of your biggest allies. Consumed in moderation, these are the foods that, for most of us, create that sense of satisfaction following a meal. Some carbohydrates, such as sugars, are quickly digested and may only satisfy you for as little as 30 minutes. Other carbohydrates, such as starches, may last up to two hours. But by adding the right amounts of protein and fats to the mix, you can extend the length of time you'll feel satisfied to up to six hours or more! By maintaining the proper balance of protein, carbs, and fat you'll be able to feel satisfied after each meal, and remain satisfied longer between meals.

Just bear in mind that with this flexibility comes accountability. The difference between losing one pound of fat a month and not losing any may be a mere 100 calories a day. That's not very much food—taking those two extra bites of potato, picking off the kid's plate while you're cleaning up, or not letting something "go to waste" is all it takes to undermine your results. Always try to focus clearly on what is enough.

> "I try to get my daily servings of fruits and vegetables, watch my fat and sugar intake, and take a daily multivitamin. But it wasn't until I started regularly working out with weights that I started to notice the difference. Wow! What a difference it has made. My arms are tight and toned; I love my biceps! I've even started to notice a difference in my glutes and hamstrings."
> **Tiffany, age 32**
> **Pittsburgh, PA**

Physical vs. Emotional Urges

Hunger is an anxious state caused by a physical need; when we eat, we feel better. Eating is the appropriate response to our physical need. The problem comes when we use eating as our response to other forms of anxiety. If we feel anxious—as we frequently may—for reasons unrelated to hunger, eating doesn't really relieve it. That unrelieved anxiety may then prompt us to eat more and more, trying to make ourselves feel better. Most of the time, though, we just end up feeling even worse than we started as a result of overeating.

You only feel true hunger when your body needs more energy. To help you get in touch with your energy needs, and begin to distinguish them from more emotionally based urges to eat, I've included a Nutritional Journal as part of your training plan. The Nutritional Journal provides space to record details about your meals: what foods you ate, at what time, and how hungry you felt beforehand. Reflecting on your level of hunger before each meal, and keeping a record of it, will help you learn how to schedule your meals to avoid becoming overly hungry, and therefore overeating. Noticing how your emotional state affects the picture will help you become more discriminating about your physical needs.

Estimating Food Portions

While being aware of your hunger level is the best way to monitor your food intake, it's also helpful to learn to recognize portion sizes. When you first start my program, I recommend measuring out the various portions in the 1-2-3 Food Table, just to see what they look like. It's not necessary to measure your food every time you eat. Doing it once or twice will give you a visual reference that should enable you to make accurate estimates from then on.

I've also found that associating the recommended portion of a food with a common object helps me gauge the amount I'm going to eat, especially when the portion is measured by weight, such as "4 oz. chicken." Use the following memory aids, or, after measuring the portions, create your own.

Pay special attention to the portions of starches and fats. Because those nutrients contain relatively more calories, small variations in portion size can make a big difference.

FOOD/PORTION	APPROXIMATE SIZE
3–4 oz. meat or fish	deck of cards
1 cup cooked vegetables	baseball
1 oz. bread	sandwich-size slice
1 oz. cheese	wine cork
1 tablespoon butter	⅔ of a standard butter pat

Your Eating Plan: Easy As 1, 2, 3!

Now we come to the basic framework you'll use to put together your meals. In the table that follows, foods are divided in three columns. To put together a meal, all you have to do is pick one food from each category. The foods and portions listed are designed to add up to meals of approximately 300–400 calories, which will give you a daily intake of about 1,500 calories, spread out over four meals. (For your convenience, this table is reproduced at the beginning of the Nutritional Journal.)

CATEGORY #1 PROTEIN	CATEGORY #2 FRUIT/VEGETABLE	CATEGORY #3 STARCH
2 eggs*	1½ cups cooked vegetables (except corn and peas)	1 slice bread; 1 small pancake; 1 frozen waffle; ¼ bagel; or 1 oz. biscuit
1 cup 2% cottage cheese; 4 oz. low-fat milk; or 4 oz. low-fat yogurt (plus ½ portion of any other protein in category)	3 cups mixed green salad with raw vegetables	½ cup rice, noodles, or pasta with tomato sauce
4 oz. lean pork, beef, turkey, or chicken	¾ cup cooked vegetables (except corn and peas) and small side salad with raw vegetables	½ cup potato, yams, cooked beans, lentils, peas, or corn
6 oz. any fish or seafood	¾ cup corn or peas	1 oz. dry cereal
2 tbs. any type nut butter*	1 cup vegetable-based soup	1 6-inch corn or nonfat flour tortilla
2 oz. low-fat cheese*	1 cup fruit salad or 1 medium piece of fruit	½ oz. (about 4–6) low-fat crackers, chips, or pretzels
1 cup soybeans, tofu, or tempeh	1 oz. dried fruit	2 cups air-popped popcorn
1 oz. nuts or seeds*		

*These foods are naturally higher in fat, so they'll fulfill your fat allowance for any meal in which they're eaten. See below for more information about fats.

Feel free to be creative with your meals by combining different types of food from the same category to reach the recommended portion. In other words, instead of one item from category #1, you may want to pick two items and cut the designated portions in half.

What About Fats?

Fat is an important part of my eating plan, and may contribute up to 30 percent of a meal's calories. The catch is that many foods—animal proteins in particular—naturally contain certain amounts of fat. For this reason, be cautious about adding more. As a guideline, it's okay to add one fat from the list below to each meal, unless your food choices are naturally higher in fat. Such foods are marked in the table with an asterisk (*).

FATS

- 1 teaspoon oil, **mayonnaise,** margarine, butter (or 2 teaspoons "lite" or low-fat versions).
- 1 tablespoon **salad dressing,** sour cream, **guacamole,** cream cheese, gravy, pesto, Alfredo sauce (or 2 tablespoons "lite" or low-fat versions).

Note: If possible, try to use the choices listed in bold type. These are good sources of healthier, unsaturated fats.

My 1-2-3 Plan will give you a simple outline within which you can feel free to be flexible and creative. In time, the good habits you acquire on this plan will become second nature, and you can move beyond the food choices on the table. Eating is more than just nutrition; it's a social and cultural experience. Enjoy it!

As you experiment with this new way of eating, notice how your body responds. Focus on your appetite, and on how the food makes you feel—both while eating and afterward. If you've been accustomed to eating cereals, bread, muffins, or bagels for breakfast, this low-starch approach will be a dramatic change. And if you're someone who regularly skips breakfast, you'll notice a significant increase in your energy levels throughout the day.

Beverages

What should you drink? I'm a strong champion of water. I recommend that you drink eight 8-ounce glasses of water a day. In addition, you may drink flavored (but not sweetened) mineral or sparkling waters. Iced or hot tea and coffee, as well as other sugar-free, noncalorie beverages (such as diet sodas) are also options.

Calorie-filled beverages such as juices and regular sodas are mostly carbohydrate in the form of sugars. Drinking them occasionally is fine, but consuming them regularly will probably slow your results. Nonfat and low-fat milk can be easily accommodated as part of your protein intake.

A word of caution concerning coffee and tea: Some people are especially sensitive to caffeine. It can make you feel jittery and unsettled, disrupt your sleep patterns, make you feel less satisfied with your food and more likely to crave sugar and sweets. Caffeine is not prohibited in this program but, to facilitate weight management, I recommend moderation.

Alcoholic beverages, too, can have negative effects on your sleep patterns and glucose levels. But, more importantly, they contribute additional calories that are likely to be stored as fat! An occasional glass of wine or beer is perfectly okay—but daily consumption may interfere with reaching your weight management goals.

Desserts

You'll notice there's no dessert column on the 1-2-3 Food Table. Well, I'm not asking you to give up desserts altogether! However, let's face it: Most desserts are rich sources of fat and sugar and need to be handled carefully.

First, don't be misled by the excitement about no-fat and low-fat desserts—excessive sugar in these foods can still present a problem. Too many people think that if a dessert contains no or little fat, they're free to eat all they want! I have found this to be a real trap. I've also found that, most of the time, lower-fat desserts don't measure up to the real thing. I think we end up eating more because we're not getting the taste satisfaction we're looking for.

For this reason, I heartily endorse eating delicious, *real* desserts! The point is to eat them *responsibly*. Maybe one or two desserts a week is all your body can handle. Here's a good strategy to use: When you know you want dessert, try to eat less starch at your meal (potatoes, rice, pasta). That way, you leave room in your carbohydrate quota for your dessert.

Sugar Cravings

Eating less sugar may be a challenge for those in the habit of eating desserts or sucking on sugar candies throughout the day. While you experiment with how many desserts you can handle (or do without), try to notice

> *"It was not easy at first, but each day I went a little further. . . . The weight came off, and I dropped two dress sizes in 3 months. My body is more toned now than it was when I was in my twenties. I also can eat more without having to worry about every ounce going straight to my hips. I have more energy than ever before and I love the way I look. Weights will not make you 'big and bulky,' but they will tone and tighten."*
> Julie, age 38
> Lehighton, PA

what happens when you start eating less sugar. Do you crave it? Do you feel bad if you don't eat it?

For some people, a little bit of sugar each day will pose no problem. For others, sugar is a time bomb waiting to go off. Consuming even a little sugar can set off cravings that get more and more intense—to the point where you may wonder if you are actually addicted to sugar!

To lessen these sugar cravings, try eating more protein, fruit, and vegetables. Usually this intense desire for sweets will quiet after three to four days of managed eating. If you suddenly realize that you've eaten lots of sugar or desserts for several days in a row, don't be surprised if those old cravings come back to haunt you. Again, raising your intake of protein, fruits, and vegetables while minimizing your sugar intake will help you stabilize. This is one case where 100 more calories from healthy food is far better than 25 calories of sugar and fat from a Hershey's Kiss.

Independence Means Choice

With a little practice, you should be able to use the principles in this chapter to take charge of your eating for yourself, making healthy choices at each meal. Feel free to experiment. Consider each meal a series of options. When you get good results from a meal—that is, when you feel satisfied and you know your nutritional needs have been met—you can make a note that that option was a keeper. And when a meal doesn't work,

1-2-3 PLAN AT A GLANCE

- Eat four meals a day, every 3 to 4 waking hours.
- Eat your first meal within two hours of waking.
- At each meal, select one choice from each category in the 1-2-3 Food Table.
- Plan ahead. Think about your day and take food with you if necessary. If you eat out, stick with the foods in the table.
- Limit intake of additional fats.
- Choose unsaturated fats over saturated fats.
- Drink 8 glasses of water a day.
- Feel free to make substitutions to the plan, staying within the basic guidelines:

  - Approx. 1,500 total calories per day
  - 25–30 percent protein
  - 45–50 percent carbohydrate (fruits/vegetables/starches)
  - 25–30 percent fat

make a note of that, too. While I love to experiment, I try to avoid making mistakes I've made in the past, and I love repeating successes.

Using Your Nutritional Journal

The Nutritional Journal that follows is a simple tool to help you become more conscious of your eating patterns. Not only will it keep you accountable for your choices, but it will also provide a useful record that will help you make better choices over time. I recommend keeping your Nutritional Journal for at least two weeks, and I've provided room for 14 days of entries. (If you'd like to keep it for a longer time, you can copy the pages and start a separate binder.)

Use the 1-2-3 Food Table at the beginning of the journal to plan your menus; after you eat, record your meals and the times you ate them. Before each meal, reflect on your level of hunger and record it in the appropriate space. This will help you learn to schedule your meals in a way that will keep your energy level constant throughout the day.

I recommend you use the "Comments" space to make note of any *emotions* that seem to be associated with your desire to eat. Recording emotional states alongside your hunger level will help uncover how much overlap there is (or isn't) between your desire to eat and your objective hunger level. Over time, this awareness will help you make a conscious distinction between emotional needs and physical ones. By doing so, you will have transformed what was once an unconscious urge to eat into a conscious choice—to eat, or not to eat. *That* is the first step toward becoming an independent eater.

Nutritional Journal

Your Eating Plan: Easy As 1, 2, 3!

In the table below, foods are divided in three columns. To put together a meal, all you have to do is pick one food from each category. The foods and portions listed are designed to add up to meals of approximately 300–400 calories (or about 1,500 calories/day), and will provide the necessary nutrients in the proper proportions. **For each of your four meals during the day, select 1 protein, 1 fruit or vegetable, and 1 starch.**

CATEGORY #1 PROTEIN	CATEGORY #2 FRUIT/VEGETABLE	CATEGORY #3 STARCH
2 eggs*	1½ cups cooked vegetables (except corn and peas)	1 slice bread; 1 small pancake; 1 frozen waffle; ¼ bagel; or 1 oz. biscuit
1 cup 2% cottage cheese; 4 oz. low-fat milk; or 4 oz. low-fat yogurt (plus ½ portion of any other protein in category)	3 cups mixed green salad with raw vegetables	½ cup rice, noodles, or pasta with tomato sauce
4 oz. lean pork, beef, turkey, or chicken	¾ cup cooked vegetables (except corn and peas) and small side salad with raw vegetables	½ cup potato, yams, cooked beans, lentils, peas, or corn
6 oz. any fish or seafood	¾ cup corn or peas	1 oz. dry cereal
2 tbs. any type nut butter*	1 cup vegetable-based soup	1 6-inch corn or nonfat flour tortilla
2 oz. low-fat cheese*	1 cup fruit salad or 1 medium piece of fruit	½ oz. (about 4–6) low-fat crackers, chips, or pretzels
1 cup soybeans, tofu, or tempeh	1 oz. dried fruit	2 cups air-popped popcorn
1 oz. nuts or seeds*		

*These foods are naturally higher in fat. Whenever you put together a meal that does *not* contain one of these higher-fat proteins, it's okay to include one fat from the list below.

FATS

- 1 teaspoon oil, **mayonnaise,** margarine, butter (or 2 teaspoons "lite" or low-fat versions).

- 1 tablespoon **salad dressing,** sour cream, **guacamole,** cream cheese, gravy, pesto, Alfredo sauce (or 2 tablespoons "lite" or low-fat versions).

Note: If possible, try to use the choices listed in bold type. These are good sources of healthier, unsaturated fats.

MONDAY

FOOD SELECTION

Date: _____
Cardio ☐
Activity _____ Min. _____

Stretching ☐

Strength Training ☐

Water (Drink 8 glasses)

○ ○ ○ ○ ○ ○ ○ ○

Comments:

Meal 1:
___ AM
___ PM

P	5	High
	4	
F/V	3	
	2	
S	1	Low

Meal 2:
___ AM
___ PM

P	5	High
	4	
F/V	3	
	2	
S	1	Low

Meal 3:
___ AM
___ PM

P	5	High
	4	
F/V	3	
	2	
S	1	Low

Meal 4:
___ AM
___ PM

P	5	High
	4	
F/V	3	
	2	
S	1	Low

TUESDAY

FOOD SELECTION

Date: _____
Cardio ☐
Activity _____ Min. _____

Stretching ☐

Strength Training ☐

Water (Drink 8 glasses)

○ ○ ○ ○ ○ ○ ○ ○

Comments:

Meal 1:
___ AM
___ PM

P	5	High
	4	
F/V	3	
	2	
S	1	Low

Meal 2:
___ AM
___ PM

P	5	High
	4	
F/V	3	
	2	
S	1	Low

Meal 3:
___ AM
___ PM

P	5	High
	4	
F/V	3	
	2	
S	1	Low

Meal 4:
___ AM
___ PM

P	5	High
	4	
F/V	3	
	2	
S	1	Low

WEDNESDAY

FOOD SELECTION

HUNGER LEVEL BEFORE MEAL

Date: _____
Cardio ☐
Activity _____ Min. _____

Stretching ☐

Strength Training ☐

Water (Drink 8 glasses)

◯◯◯◯◯◯◯◯

Comments:

Meal 1:		Hunger
___ AM ___ PM	P	5 High / 4
	F/V	3 / 2
	S	1 Low

Meal 2:		
___ AM ___ PM	P	5 High / 4
	F/V	3 / 2
	S	1 Low

Meal 3:		
___ AM ___ PM	P	5 High / 4
	F/V	3 / 2
	S	1 Low

Meal 4:		
___ AM ___ PM	P	5 High / 4
	F/V	3 / 2
	S	1 Low

THURSDAY

FOOD SELECTION

HUNGER LEVEL BEFORE MEAL

Date: _____
Cardio ☐
Activity _____ Min. _____

Stretching ☐

Strength Training ☐

Water (Drink 8 glasses)

◯◯◯◯◯◯◯◯

Comments:

Meal 1:		
___ AM ___ PM	P	5 High / 4
	F/V	3 / 2
	S	1 Low

Meal 2:		
___ AM ___ PM	P	5 High / 4
	F/V	3 / 2
	S	1 Low

Meal 3:		
___ AM ___ PM	P	5 High / 4
	F/V	3 / 2
	S	1 Low

Meal 4:		
___ AM ___ PM	P	5 High / 4
	F/V	3 / 2
	S	1 Low

FRIDAY

Date: _____
Cardio ❑
Activity _____ Min. _____

Stretching ❑

Strength Training ❑

Water (Drink 8 glasses)

○ ○ ○ ○ ○ ○ ○ ○
Comments:

FOOD SELECTION	HUNGER LEVEL BEFORE MEAL

Meal 1:
___ AM
___ PM

P	5 High
	4
F/V	3
	2
S	1 Low

Meal 2:
___ AM
___ PM

P	5 High
	4
F/V	3
	2
S	1 Low

Meal 3:
___ AM
___ PM

P	5 High
	4
F/V	3
	2
S	1 Low

Meal 4:
___ AM
___ PM

P	5 High
	4
F/V	3
	2
S	1 Low

SATURDAY

Date: _____
Cardio ❑
Activity _____ Min. _____

Stretching ❑

Strength Training ❑

Water (Drink 8 glasses)

○ ○ ○ ○ ○ ○ ○ ○
Comments:

FOOD SELECTION	HUNGER LEVEL BEFORE MEAL

Meal 1:
___ AM
___ PM

P	5 High
	4
F/V	3
	2
S	1 Low

Meal 2:
___ AM
___ PM

P	5 High
	4
F/V	3
	2
S	1 Low

Meal 3:
___ AM
___ PM

P	5 High
	4
F/V	3
	2
S	1 Low

Meal 4:
___ AM
___ PM

P	5 High
	4
F/V	3
	2
S	1 Low

SUNDAY

| | FOOD SELECTION | HUNGER LEVEL BEFORE MEAL |

Date: _____
Cardio ☐
Activity _____ Min. _____

Stretching ☐

Strength Training ☐

Water (Drink 8 glasses)

○ ○ ○ ○ ○ ○ ○

Comments:

Meal 1:
___ AM
___ PM

P	
F/V	
S	

5	High
4	
3	
2	
1	Low

Meal 2:
___ AM
___ PM

P	
F/V	
S	

5	High
4	
3	
2	
1	Low

Meal 3:
___ AM
___ PM

P	
F/V	
S	

5	High
4	
3	
2	
1	Low

Meal 4:
___ AM
___ PM

P	
F/V	
S	

5	High
4	
3	
2	
1	Low

MONDAY

| | FOOD SELECTION | HUNGER LEVEL BEFORE MEAL |

Date: _____
Cardio ☐
Activity _____ Min. _____

Stretching ☐

Strength Training ☐

Water (Drink 8 glasses)

○ ○ ○ ○ ○ ○ ○

Comments:

Meal 1:
___ AM
___ PM

P	
F/V	
S	

5	High
4	
3	
2	
1	Low

Meal 2:
___ AM
___ PM

P	
F/V	
S	

5	High
4	
3	
2	
1	Low

Meal 3:
___ AM
___ PM

P	
F/V	
S	

5	High
4	
3	
2	
1	Low

Meal 4:
___ AM
___ PM

P	
F/V	
S	

5	High
4	
3	
2	
1	Low

TUESDAY

| | FOOD SELECTION | HUNGER LEVEL BEFORE MEAL |

Date: _____
Cardio ☐
Activity _____ Min. _____

Stretching ☐

Strength Training ☐

Water (Drink 8 glasses)

○ ○ ○ ○ ○ ○ ○ ○

Comments:

Meal 1:
___ AM
___ PM

P		5 High
		4
F/V		3
		2
S		1 Low

Meal 2:
___ AM
___ PM

P		5 High
		4
F/V		3
		2
S		1 Low

Meal 3:
___ AM
___ PM

P		5 High
		4
F/V		3
		2
S		1 Low

Meal 4:
___ AM
___ PM

P		5 High
		4
F/V		3
		2
S		1 Low

WEDNESDAY

| | FOOD SELECTION | HUNGER LEVEL BEFORE MEAL |

Date: _____
Cardio ☐
Activity _____ Min. _____

Stretching ☐

Strength Training ☐

Water (Drink 8 glasses)

○ ○ ○ ○ ○ ○ ○ ○

Comments:

Meal 1:
___ AM
___ PM

P		5 High
		4
F/V		3
		2
S		1 Low

Meal 2:
___ AM
___ PM

P		5 High
		4
F/V		3
		2
S		1 Low

Meal 3:
___ AM
___ PM

P		5 High
		4
F/V		3
		2
S		1 Low

Meal 4:
___ AM
___ PM

P		5 High
		4
F/V		3
		2
S		1 Low

THURSDAY

| | FOOD SELECTION | HUNGER LEVEL BEFORE MEAL |

Date: _____
Cardio ❑
Activity _____ Min. _____

Stretching ❑

Strength Training ❑

Water (Drink 8 glasses)

◯◯◯◯◯◯◯

Comments:

Meal 1:
___ AM
___ PM

P	5 High
	4
F/V	3
	2
S	1 Low

Meal 2:
___ AM
___ PM

P	5 High
	4
F/V	3
	2
S	1 Low

Meal 3:
___ AM
___ PM

P	5 High
	4
F/V	3
	2
S	1 Low

Meal 4:
___ AM
___ PM

P	5 High
	4
F/V	3
	2
S	1 Low

FRIDAY

| | FOOD SELECTION | HUNGER LEVEL BEFORE MEAL |

Date: _____
Cardio ❑
Activity _____ Min. _____

Stretching ❑

Strength Training ❑

Water (Drink 8 glasses)

◯◯◯◯◯◯◯

Comments:

Meal 1:
___ AM
___ PM

P	5 High
	4
F/V	3
	2
S	1 Low

Meal 2:
___ AM
___ PM

P	5 High
	4
F/V	3
	2
S	1 Low

Meal 3:
___ AM
___ PM

P	5 High
	4
F/V	3
	2
S	1 Low

Meal 4:
___ AM
___ PM

P	5 High
	4
F/V	3
	2
S	1 Low

SATURDAY

| | FOOD SELECTION | HUNGER LEVEL BEFORE MEAL |

Date: _____

Cardio ☐

Activity _____ Min. _____

Stretching ☐

Strength Training ☐

Water (Drink 8 glasses)

○ ○ ○ ○ ○ ○ ○ ○

Comments:

Meal 1:
___ AM
___ PM

P

F/V

S

5 High
4
3
2
1 Low

Meal 2:
___ AM
___ PM

P

F/V

S

5 High
4
3
2
1 Low

Meal 3:
___ AM
___ PM

P

F/V

S

5 High
4
3
2
1 Low

Meal 4:
___ AM
___ PM

P

F/V

S

5 High
4
3
2
1 Low

SUNDAY

| | FOOD SELECTION | HUNGER LEVEL BEFORE MEAL |

Date: _____

Cardio ☐

Activity _____ Min. _____

Stretching ☐

Strength Training ☐

Water (Drink 8 glasses)

○ ○ ○ ○ ○ ○ ○ ○

Comments:

Meal 1:
___ AM
___ PM

P

F/V

S

5 High
4
3
2
1 Low

Meal 2:
___ AM
___ PM

P

F/V

S

5 High
4
3
2
1 Low

Meal 3:
___ AM
___ PM

P

F/V

S

5 High
4
3
2
1 Low

Meal 4:
___ AM
___ PM

P

F/V

S

5 High
4
3
2
1 Low

Chapter 12

A Lifetime Prescription

Suppose you had awakened this morning with the body of your dreams. Now what? Well, no matter how perfect it might be, that body would immediately fall prey to the influences of time and gravity, excess calories, inactivity, and other lifestyle factors. Your perfect physique would stay that way only as long as you worked to maintain it. That's why the "quick fix" is a myth. Lifelong health is a lifelong project.

In this book, we've covered everything you need to know to experience the exciting benefits of strength training. A short twelve weeks from now, you'll be feeling stronger and leaner, with a new sense of vitality sparking through your body. In closing, I'd like to take a few moments to put this in the context of an overall formula for a healthy lifestyle.

Looking Ahead

As we've seen, strength training offers benefits to women of all ages. If you're in your twenties, lifting weights will improve sports performance, create a leaner body composition, and help build more attractive muscle contour. Women approaching 40, however, get these benefits and *more*. The older we get, the more dramatic the health benefits of exercise become. Strength training—and other types of exercise—become vital for maintaining functional strength, a healthy heart, and strong bones. In other words, fitness matters more and more.

I don't know about you, but when I'm in my sixties and seventies, I want to be up, doing things, and having an active life. Strength training is definitely one of the things that can ensure that. Still, there are other parts to the picture as well. I want to leave you with a simple, overall formula for achieving a healthy, well-balanced state of fitness and maintaining it over the years to come.

Kathy's Lifetime Prescription

There are four components to good physical fitness: **muscular strength**, **lean body composition**, **cardiorespiratory endurance,** and **flexibility.** In this book, we've covered how to build muscular strength and improve body composition through lifting weights. We've also covered flexibility training, and I've given you a simple plan for healthy eating. To round out your fitness program, I recommend doing some form of aerobic exercise to keep your heart strong and help burn calories.

This may sound like a lot, but it doesn't have to be. Of course, people's bodies respond differently, and different training goals will dictate modifications to this approach. But if you're looking for a place to start—and a simple program you can live with—here's a good, basic formula for lifelong fitness:

> "Since I've added weight training to my exercise regimen, my metabolism has increased and my body is much firmer. My friends tell me I look like I did when I was in college. Of course, eating a healthy diet and doing aerobic exercise are key, but the weight training gives me the added edge I need to continue on to the next level of fitness."
> Christine, age 32
> Kenner, LA

Strength Training

Strength-train 2 to 3 days a week for 20 to 30 minutes. (In the early phase of this program, 20 minutes twice a week is all you'll need.)

Aerobics

Exercise aerobically a minimum of 3 days a week for 30 minutes. Accumulate total minutes any way possible. For example, three 10-minute sessions provide similar benefits to one 30-minute workout. (Again, the exact length of time will depend on your goals. If you have a lot of excess weight to lose, or you want to get in shape to run a marathon, you'd need to increase your aerobic quota by working out more days, for longer periods.)

Flexibility

Stretch all your major muscle groups once a day using the ten-stretch program in this book.

Nutrition

Follow the 1-2-3 Plan in Chapter 11.

A Sample Week

Here's an example of how a week might look, following this simple formula:

MON	TUES	WED	THURS	FRI	SAT	SUN
Cardio (30 min)		Cardio (30 min)		Cardio (30 min)		Rest
	Strength		Strength		Strength	
Stretch	Stretch	Stretch	Stretch	Stretch	Stretch	

Remember, it's not necessary to try to change everything in your life at once. Adopt this formula by degrees. Spend plenty of time noticing and celebrating the positive changes you feel at each step of the way. You can help reinforce this fitness regimen by making what I call healthy choices in all areas of your life.

Making Healthy Choices

Healthy choices are the tiny moments of truth that happen all through the day, when you decide to pass on that last doughnut, or take a flight of stairs instead of the elevator. The choices you make in juggling your schedule to find time to work out, the decision to walk the dog instead of watching TV—it's the little things! Just keep asking yourself if the choice you're making—no matter how small—is pointing you in the direction you want to go. Every choice counts!

- **Make healthy food choices.**

Avoid high-calorie fast food by packing yourself a healthy lunch in the morning. I make it a habit whenever I'm away from home for a few hours to carry an "emergency kit" in my car, containing some water, a piece of fruit, and half a peanut butter sandwich. That way, I know I won't have to rely on fast food and vending machines during the day. And when you sit down to a meal, remind yourself that there will always be a *next* meal, so there's no need to gorge yourself at this one. Feel free to walk down a buffet line without taking everything!

- **Find nonchemical means to change your state.**

I've noticed that many of my peers have reached a stage in their lives where their answer to problems is some form of medication: drugs for depression, drugs for menopause, drugs for PMS. My suggestion is: Make healthy choices your first resort. You'll be surprised how seldom you need to look any further for relief. Got a headache? Instead of immediately popping two aspirin, how about drinking a big glass of water and then doing 15 minutes of stretching to work out the tension in your neck and shoulders? Hitting that mid-afternoon wall? Instead of another cup of coffee, how about a 5-minute catnap or a brisk walk? Insomnia? Try a hot bath, a foot massage, or a little stretching before bed. Instead of relying on chemicals to change your state, focus on self-reliance and natural solutions.

- **Look for creative ways to make exercise a part of your daily life.**

Take a couple flights of stairs instead of waiting 4 minutes for the elevator. Walk short distances instead of driving. Plan active get-togethers with friends: Instead of meeting for lunch, go for a hike or a bike ride.

- **Business trips and vacations: plan ahead!**

Most hotels or conference organizers are prepared to steer you toward local exercise facilities. Call ahead and ask questions. Does your hotel have a weight room? A pool? Are there good jogging trails nearby? Could you walk from the hotel to the meeting area, or from there to lunch? Is there a health club nearby that offers daily or weekly memberships? (Most do.) Activity doesn't have to be structured: Sightseeing provides plenty of opportunity for brisk walking and climbing hills or stairs.

- **Take an active vacation.**

If you're feeling ambitious, there are many types of active vacations available—everything from white-water rafting to bicycling tours through California wine country. Having a romantic adventure to look forward to is a great way to motivate yourself to do a little training. Various travel companies offer all-inclusive packages. Other active vacation options include hikes, canoeing, kayaking, rafting, or various multisport packages.

• Stop trying to be perfect.

Lowering your expectations for yourself and your performance is a good way to relieve feelings of stress, and often results in doing better. Once you've decided it's okay not to be perfect, you'll find yourself enjoying your life far more. Everything you do doesn't have to be a 10.

• Find healthier, more balanced ways to feel good about yourself.

We live in a society where material possessions or the appearance of perfection are marks of success. But the people I really admire are the ones who have found a balance: They love their work, they do their best, but they also make time to go walking in the mountains with their dog. They've found a way to make a contribution to society while staying focused on the things that matter: their relationships with loved ones, with nature, and with some form of spirituality—to me, that's a life worth living. I've helped you simplify your workout; my advice to you is to find ways to simplify your life!

A Body in Motion

I've thought a lot about people's patterns when it comes to taking care of themselves. The physical principles of momentum and inertia seem to apply: As Newton said, a body in motion tends to stay in motion. Once it stops, it's much tougher to budge.

When you first start training, the system usually works for a while. You see results, you start to feel good about yourself, and this creates momentum. Then, something happens. You come down with the flu. House guests arrive. Some overload of activities interrupts the flow—holidays, business…you're juggling too many demands, too many deadlines. Like a spinning top that's started to wobble, you lose your equilibrium and everything tumbles to a halt.

If your program stops for a week, or even two, you're usually okay. But if it stops for much longer, you lose momentum. At this point, it's almost inevitable that you'll wind back down and have to start again.

> "At 74, my waist, which was disappearing, has made a remarkable recovery and my posture has improved. Just as important, my energy level and attitude have improved. What's more, I feel good about myself, even when I look in a mirror. You can't beat that, can you?"
> Marion
> Houston, TX

Managing the Cycles

Cycles are normal. Just as plants have dormant seasons, and animals hibernate, your energy level will fluctuate, not only daily, but on a seasonal basis, too. The trick is to *manage* the cycles: Find ways to shorten the period between the up phases so you don't stay down too long. Two secrets:

• *Be more moderate during the up phase.* People who've made a sudden decision to get in shape often stack the deck against themselves by taking on too much. Working out for an hour and a half every day quickly becomes a burden. They either burn themselves out, or they abandon it because it's just too time consuming. Even if you're feeling highly motivated, keeping your commitment moderate will help ensure long-term success.

• *When you feel the pressure, cut yourself some slack!* Imagine a sailboat streaking through the water: When you feel the force of the wind building, you have to loosen up on the sail or the rudder. Otherwise, the wind pushes the boat over and you end up in the water. Maintain your program during the hectic times, like holidays or exams, by scaling it back so it doesn't collapse. Do this as a proactive measure, at the first sign of pressure. Lower your expectations, but don't stop completely, because that's when inertia sets in. If I'm in a real crunch period, I might limit my workouts to 10 minutes a day. When the crunch is over, I expand them again. Do whatever it takes to keep that body in motion!

A Lifetime of Rewards

> *"[Weight training] takes dedication and a lot of hard work, but it is well worth it. I feel better physically than I ever have in my life. I now realize that how much you weigh isn't nearly as important as how you feel!"*
> Sharon
> Avondale, AZ

Throughout my years as a fitness educator, people have told me they found exercise to be boring, time consuming, and hard work—but no one has *ever* told me it wasn't beneficial! I'm sure if I could offer the benefits of exercise in pill form, people would be swallowing it like candy. Everyone is sold on the *idea* of exercise. The thing that holds us back is the work involved.

Work, though, is the mainspring of our lives. It's the principle force behind so much of what's really valuable. Relationships, creative endeavors, schooling—these all require effort, yet we pursue them anyway, because of their importance to our overall happiness and well-being. I've done my best to simplify for you the challenge of living a more active life. If you can start to view exercise as play, or social time, or even as revitalizing therapy, it will help you shift your focus from the work to the rewards. I'm not saying it's easy to change your thinking—even that takes work!—but I *am* saying it's the key to much of the pleasure in life!

I hope you'll use the information in this book to obtain the rewards that I *know* are waiting for you from living a healthier, more active life.

Kathy Smith's Lift Weights to Lose Weight 12-Week Promise

Yes! I'm convinced of the benefits of lifting weights and I'm ready to experience them for myself. I will follow the Kathy Smith *Lift Weights to Lose Weight* plan for the next 12 weeks. I will establish a place to work out—either at home or in a gym—and I will do at least 2 strength training workouts each week. I understand that when I successfully complete this 12-week introduction, and notify Kathy by sending in the Completion Stub on page 283 I will qualify to have my name appear on the Kathy Smith *Lift Weights to Lose Weight* Honor Roll at www.KathySmith.com.

Date: _____

Signed: _____

Name: _____

Address: _____

Telephone: _____

E-mail: _____

Accountability Booster: I'm sending this signed pledge to Kathy to hold while I complete the 12-week program.

Send to:
Kathy Smith Lifestyles
PO Box 491433
Los Angeles CA 90049

Send this form to Kathy Smith Lifestyles after you've completed your 12-week introduction.

Completion Stub

I did it! This is to notify Kathy Smith Lifestyles that I have followed through on my 12-week pledge to myself and successfully completed my introduction to strength training. Please place my name on the Kathy Smith *Lift Weights to Lose Weight* Honor Roll at www.KathySmith.com.

Date: _____

Signed: _____

Name: _____

Address: _____

Telephone: _____

E-mail: _____

Comments about my strength training experience:

_____

_____

_____

_____

_____

_____

_____

_____

_____

_____

Send to:
Kathy Smith Lifestyles
PO Box 491433
Los Angeles CA 90049

Meal Planner

Here's a handy shopping template to help streamline your food buying. Make as many photocopies of these pages as you need. Keep a copy handy during the week and mark down items as you think of them; when you go to the market, take the list with you.

**PROTEIN
SOURCES**
Meats and Poultry
Beef
Chicken
Ground meat (beef,
   chicken, turkey)
Pork
Sliced meat (turkey,
   ham, beef)
Other deli meats: _____
Other meats: _____

Fish and Seafood
Cod
Halibut
Salmon
Scallops
Shrimp
Sole

Swordfish
Tuna (fresh or canned
   in water)
Other seafood: _____

Dairy
Cheese (low-fat)
Cottage cheese (low-fat)
Cream cheese (low-fat)
Eggs
Milk (low-fat, nonfat)
Other dairy: _____

**Nuts, Seeds, and
Legumes**
Almonds
Peanut butter
   (low-fat)
Peanuts
Pecans

Pine nuts
Pumpkin seeds
Sesame seeds
Sunflower seeds
Walnuts
Other nut butters
   (low-fat): _____
Other nuts and seeds:
_____

**CARBOHYDRATE
SOURCES—FRUITS
AND VEGETABLES**
**Fruits (fresh, frozen,
   canned, jarred)**
Apples
Apple sauce (apple
   butter)
Apricots
Bananas

Berries
Cantaloupe
Dates/Figs
Grapefruit
Grapes
Honeydew
Kiwi
Lemons (juice)
Limes (juice)
Mangoes
Mixed frozen fruit
Nectarines
Oranges
Papayas
Peaches
Pears
Pineapple
Plums
Prunes
Tangerines

Watermelon
Other fruits: _____

Vegetables (fresh, frozen, canned, jarred)

Alfalfa sprouts
Artichokes
Asparagus
Bamboo shoots
Bean sprouts
Beets
Black olives
Broccoli
Brussels sprouts
Cabbage
Carrots
Cauliflower
Celery
Corn
Cucumbers
Eggplant
Endive
Green beans
Leeks
Lettuces
Mixed vegetables (frozen)
Mushrooms
Onions
Parsnips
Peas
Peppers, (green/red bell, chili, jalepeño)
Potatoes
Radishes
Scallions
Spinach
Squash
Sweet potatoes
Tomatoes (whole, paste, puree, stewed)
Vegetable broth/soups
Yams
Zucchini
Other vegetables:

_____

CARBOHYDRATE SOURCES— STARCHES Bread Products and Flour (whole wheat/multigrain are best)

Bagels
Bread crumbs
Bread/rolls
Cornmeal
Croutons
Flour
Pancake/waffle mix
Pita pockets
Tortillas (corn, nonfat flour)
Waffles (frozen)
Other bread products:

_____

Pastas, Rice, and Grains

Barley
Brown rice
Couscous
Oats
Orzo
Pastas
Rice noodles
White/basmati rice
Wild rice
Other pasta, rice, and grains:_____

Beans and Legumes

Beans (all types except green)
Chick peas
Lentils (red, green)
Refried beans (low-fat)
Soybeans
Split peas
Other beans and legumes:_____

Cereals

Cream of rice

Cream of wheat
Dry cereals
Granola
Oatmeal
Other cereals: _____

CARBOHYDRATE SOURCES— SNACKS

Chips (baked, low-fat)
Crackers (fat-free)
Dried fruits
Fig/date bars
Graham crackers (low-fat)
Popcorn
Pretzels
Raisins
Rice cakes
Vegetables (cleaned, pre-cut)
Other snack foods:

_____

FATS AND OILS

Butter
Cooking spray (natural, nonfat)
Corn oil
Margarine
Olive oil
Safflower oil
Other oils: _____

SPICES

Allspice
Basil
Black pepper
Cinnamon
Garlic (fresh, jarred, salt, powder)
Ginger (fresh, powder)
Oregano
Paprika
Rosemary
Seasoned salt
Tarragon
Thyme

Other spices: _____

Condiments

Barbecue sauce
Fruit jams/spreads (all fruit)
Honey
Horseradish
Ketchup
Maple syrup (pure)
Mayonnaise (low-fat, eggless)
Mustard (whole grain)
Pasta sauce
Pickles
Relish
Salad dressings (low-fat)
Salsa
Soy sauce (low-salt)
Tabasco sauce
Vinegar
Worcestershire sauce
Other condiments:

_____

BEVERAGES

Fruit juices (fresh, frozen)
Herb teas
Natural sodas
Sparkling water
Spring water
Other beverages:

_____

MISC: _____

_____

_____

_____

_____

_____

_____

_____

_____

_____

Page numbers of photos and illustrations appear in italics

Ab (abdominal) exercises, 134–43
  assisted ab curl-up, 138
  combo ab curl, 136, *137*
  curl-up, 134, *135*
  sequence of, 52
  variety option: oblique ab curl, 140, *141*
  variety option: reverse ab curl, 142, *143*
Aerobic exercise
  antidepressant effect, 14
  cardio recommendations, 12 week program, 226, 228, 230, 232, 234, 236, 238, 240, 242, 244, 246, 248
  heart health and, 14
  impact and, 12
  lifetime prescription, 274–75
  lower body and, 3
  muscle tone and, 1
  upper body and, 3
  warming up with, 87
  weight loss and, 1
Alcoholic beverages, 261
Anabolic steroids, 6
Arm exercises. *See also* Biceps; Shoulders; Stretches; Triceps
  biceps, 146–55
  triceps, 158–65
  shoulder exercises, 168–73
Arms, granny, 21, 56

Back exercises, 118–31. *See also* Stretches
  gym option: cable low row, 126, *127*
  gym option: lat (laterals) pull-down machine, 69, *69*, 124, *125*
  high elbow row, 122, *123*
  low back extension, 118, *119*
  one-arm row with dumbbells, 120, *121*
  variety option: back

extension with rotation, 130, *131*
  variety option: seated back flye, 128, *129*
  warm up, 87
Back pain
  relief and strength training, 13
  stretching to prevent problems, 86–87
Balance and coordination, 12. *See also* Stabilizing exercises
Beverages, 260–61
  alcoholic, 261
  coffee and tea warning, 261
Biceps, 146–55
  curl with reverse grip, 148, *149*
  gym option: cable curl, 152, *153*
  preacher curl, 150, *151*
  sequencing, 52
  standing curl, *45*, 146, *147*
  variety option: concentration curl, 154, *155*
  warm up, 87
Body shape, 17–21
  ectomorph, 19, *19*, 22–23
  endomorph, 20, *20*, 22, 24
  factors in variations of, 18
  imaging your ideal, 18
  mesomorph, 20, *20*, 21–22, 23
  muscle contour, appearance after 12 weeks of strength training, 100
  proportions, improving, 22
  strength training for body types, 22–24
  strength training for sculpting and toning, 11, 42
  type, self-test, 21

Bone
  density, 35
  density, age and causes of loss, 2, 35–36
  osteoporosis, 36–37, 88
  strength training to reverse bone loss, 10–11
Breathing during strength training, 46
"Burn," 47, 48
Buttocks and hips, 176–91. *See also* Stretches
  gym option: leg extension machine, 184, *185*
  gym option: leg press, 182, *183*
  gym option: Smith rack lunge, 186, *187*
  hip lift with legs on chair, 176, *177*
  skier's lunge, 180, *181*
  squat holding dumbbells, 178, *179*
  variety option: front lunge, 188, *189*
  variety option: wall squat with one-leg lift, 190, *191*

Calcium, 35–36
Calories, 255–56
  burned per hour, 234
  distribution across food groups, recommended, 253
  hunger level and intake of, 255–56
  per day, 255
  per meal, 259
  restricting, 251
Carbohydrates, 253–54
  balanced diet and, 240
  benefits, 244
  cravings, 261–62
  cravings and progesterone rise, 242
  desserts, 261–62
  digestion of and hunger, 237

meal creation table, 259, 264
  reactions to various types, 236
  sweets, eating as dessert, 238, 261–62
  types, 253
Cellulite, 33, 34–35
Chest exercises, 106–15. *See also* Stretches
  flye, 110, *111*
  gym option: seated chest press machine, 112, *113*
  gym option: straight bar bench press, 114, *115*
  press with dumbbells, 106, *107*
  push-up, 108, *109*

Depression
  effect of exercise on, 14
  nonchemical treatment of, 276

Energy, increase and strength training, 13
Equipment
  barbells, 59, *59*, 67
  bench or chair, 66, *66*
  cardio equipment (treadmill or elliptical machines), 67
  dumbbells, 59, *59*, 65
  exercise balls, 67
  floor mat, 66
  personal accessories, 66
  weight machines, 60, *60*, 66–67
Estrogen, 36

Fat, body
  age, athletic bodies and leanness, 34
  age and increase in, 2
  body type and amount of 19–21, *19*, *20*
  "burning," 6
  bulkier than muscle, 4
  energy storage of, 32

Fat, body *continued*
  metabolism increase and, 10
  muscle vs., 31–33
  percentage, ideal, 33–34
  problem areas and spot reducing, 34–35
  scale deceptive about, 4
Fat, dietary, 254, 257, 260
  desserts and, 261
  meal creation table, 260, 264
Food and nutrition. *See also* Calories; Carbohydrates; Fat, dietary; Hunger and appetite; Protein
  balanced diet for more energy, 240
  benefits of carbs, 244
  beverages, 260–61
  breakfast importance, 256
  breakfast protein, 226
  caloric distribution in food groups, 253
  caloric intake recommended, 255–56
  calories burned per hour, 234
  carbohydrates, reactions to, 236
  cravings and progesterone rise, 242
  desserts, 261–62
  dieting ineffective, 251
  eating throughout the day, 256
  estimated food portions, 258
  food as tranquilizer, breaking the habit, 228
  framework for meal creation, table, 259, 264
  healthy choices, 276
  independent eater, becoming, 252
  managing your weight, eating when hungry, 230, 231
  nighttime snacking, curtailing, 247
  nutritional journal, 252, 258, 263, 265–71
  1-2-3 plan, 252–71
  1-2-3 plan, at a glance, 262
  PMS and metabolism, 232
  snacking, 248
  sweets for dessert, 238
Form, 44, *45*

Gym (outside) training, 61–62
  advantages, 61
  Kathy's favorite machines, 69–71, *69–71*
  machines vs. free weight debate, 67–69
  selecting a gym or health club, 62–63
  what to look for in, 63
Gym, home, 59, 62
  advantages, 62
  equipment needed, 65–67
  making it work, 63–65

Heart. *See also* Aerobic exercise
  aerobic exercise and, 14
  blood lipid profiles improved by strength training, 14
Hunger and appetite
  calories and, 255–56
  cravings and, 242
  eating throughout the day and, 256
  managing your weight, eating when hungry, 230, 231
  nutritional journal and, 258
  physical vs. emotional urges, 257–58
  role of, and satisfaction, 257–58

Injury
  pain of, 47
  protection and strength training, 12
  stretching to prevent, 86
Isometrics, 30, 40
  inner thigh squeeze, 216, *217*

Joints, 26
  ball-in-socket, 27
  hinge, 26
  muscles, opposing to stabilize, 50–51
  strength training to help aerobics and, 12

Lactic acid, 47
Lat (lateral) exercises. *See* Back exercises
Leg exercises, 191–209. *See also* Hip and buttock exercises; Stretches

extension machine, 70, *70, see also* Hip and buttock exercises,
  extensions, "burn" and, 47, 48
  gym option: inner/outer thigh machine, 202, *203*
  gym option: leg curl machine, 70, *70,* 200–201
  gym option: seated calf raise, 204, *205*
  one-legged heel raise, 198, *199*
  press machine, 71, *71*
  self-resisted hamstring curl, 194, *195*
  side lift with ankle weights, 196, *197*
  variety option: rear lift with ankle weights, 206, *207*
  variety option: toe raise with self-resistance, 208, *209*
Lift Weights to Lose Weight video (Smith), 8, 50
Lifetime prescription
  aerobics, 274
  flexibility, 275
  healthy choices, 275–77
  motivation and persistence, 277–78
  nutrition, 275
  sample week, 275
  strength training, 274
Ligaments, 27
Lower body workout. *See* Ab (abdominal) exercises; Buttocks and hips exercises; Leg exercises

Menopause, 3
  HRT and, 37, 276
  non-chemical treatment of, 276
  preventing bone loss and, 36–37
Metabolic rate
  age and drop in, 2
  breakfast importance, 256
  calories burned per hour, 234
  body type and, 19–20
  muscle vs. fat and, 32–33
  PMS and, 232
  strength training to increase, 10, 274

Motivation (making it happen), 73–83
  cut bite-size pieces, 80–81
  excuses, 73
  inspiring yourself, 75–76
  keep it manageable, 77–79
  lifelong prescription, and persistence, 277–78
  partner for work-out, 81–82
  payoff, 80
  prioritizing, 75
  rewards, 79
  steps to follow, 75–83
  time management, 82–83
  12-week promise, 76–77
Muscle basics
  action of muscles, 27, 30
  contraction, degree of, 30
  contraction, types of, 30, *30*
  fat vs., 31–33
  fiber, 26, 30
  fiber, color (fast twitch vs. slow twitch), 32
  interdependency, 51
  major muscle groups, *28, 29*
  motor units, 30
  pairs, 27, 50
  properties of: strength, endurance, tone, 31
  root of word, 31
  skeletal muscle, 26–27
  soreness after exercise, 27, 47–48
  tissue, types of, 26
  two-joint, 27
Muscle isolation, 46
Muscle mass, 2–3
  age and loss of, 2, 32–33
  fat replacing, 2–3
  feminine looking vs, bulk, 5–7, 8, 23, 44
  strength training and building, 33
  upper body loss, 3
  tissues associated with, 12
Muscle tone
  repetitions and, 42
  strength training and, 46
  upper body loss, 1, 3

Nautilus machines, 7–8
Nutritional journal, 252, 258, 263, 265–71

Overload, 41
Overtraining, 56–57

Pace (rest periods between sets and exercises), 43, 225
Pain
   "burn," 47, 48
   injury, 47
   sharp, with stretching, warning, 88
   soreness after exercise, 27, 47–48
Personal trainers, 8
Physical fitness, four components of, 274
PMS
   cravings and progesterone rise, 242
   and metabolism, 232
   non-chemical treatment of, 276
Positive thinking, 12
Posture
   strength training and better, 12
   stretching for, 86
Pregnancy, 3
ProBell, 65
Progression, 41–42, 49, 52
Protein, 254
   balanced diet and, 240, 257
   blood sugar rise protection, 238
   breakfast, 226
   cravings curbed by, 242, 262
   meal creation table, 259, 264
   nighttime snacking, curtailing, 247

Rear raise. See Leg exercises
Reps (repetitions), 42
   amount of weight and, 42, 43, 225
   assisted (forced), 81
   focusing, 225
   guidelines, 43, 225
   low vs. high, 42
   periodization, 55–56
   range of motion and, 225
   reaching fatigue, 225
   rest periods (between sets and exercises), 43, 225
Resistance, 40–41
   range of motion, 40–41, 225
Routine, 49–58. See also Training log
   beginners, special note, 225

exercises, summary of, 101–3
full body workout, two 20-minute sessions, 57
muscle interdependency, 51–52
periodization, 55–56
planned breaks, 58
progression: increase the intensity, 52
rest (48 hours down-time), 53–54, 225
selection and number of exercises, 50–51
stress, over-training, and rest, 56–58
time schedule and, 53, 225
variety, 54–55
work from center of body outward, 52

Scheduling, 53, 225
   managing busy times in your life and exercise, 278
   stopping and starting up again, 277–78
Self-reliance and personal power, 15
Sets, 12
Shoulder exercises, 168–73. See also Stretches
   lateral raise, 168, *169*
   overhead press, 170, *171*
   overhead press warm up, 87
   rear raise, 172, *173*
   warm ups, 87
Skin quality, improved and strength training, 13–14
Sleep, stretching to enhance, 87
Spotting, 81
Stabilizer exercises, 212–23
   face-down plank, 214, *215*
   face-up plank, 218, *219*
   isometric inner thigh squeeze, 216, *217*
   one-leg lift, 222, *223*
   pendulum, 212, *213*
   push-up position with leg lift, 220, *221*
Strength
   double in 12 weeks, 100
   functional, 46–47
   importance of, 11

improved, 33
injury protection and, 12
Strength training
   age and benefits, 273–74
   benefits, 4, 9–15
   body type, focus for each, 22–24
   exercise basics, 39–48
   exercise overview, 101–3
   hours per week required, 3
   intimidation factor, 7 8
   lifetime prescription, 274
   managing busy times in your life and, 278
   myths and misconceptions about, 6
   routine, creating your, 49–58
   stopping and starting up again, 277–78
   weight loss achieved by, 3–4
Stress
   overtraining and, 56–57
   reduction, daily workout and, 14–15
   strength-training, need to stretch to prevent, 86
   stretching to release tension, 85–86
Stretches, 85–98. See also Warm up
   active recovery, 88
   benefits, 86–87
   guidelines, 88
   front of hip/chest/front of shoulder, 92, *92*
   hamstring/calf, 89, *89*
   hamstring/side of back, 96, *96*
   hips/buttocks/lower back, 90, *90*
   inner thigh/side of back, 97, *97*
   lifetime prescription, 275
   outer hip/torso, 95, *95*
   quad/hip flexor, 94, *94*
   rear shoulder/neck, 93, *93*
   recommendations, 12 week program, 226, 228, 230, 232, 234, 236, 238, 240, 242, 244, 246, 248
   rotary torso, 91, *91*
   standing cat back/abdominal, 98, *98*

Tendons, 12, 26

Testosterone, 6
Training log, 77–78, 99, 224–49
   block 1, week 1, 226, 227
   block 1, week 2, 228, 229
   block 1, week 3, 230, 231
   block 1, week 4, 232, 233
   block 2, week 5, 234, 235
   block 2, week 6, 236, 237
   block 2, week 7, 238, 239
   block 2, week 8, 240, 241
   block 3, week 9, 242, 243
   block 3, week 10, 244, 245
   block 3, week 11, 246, 247
   block 3, week 12, 248, 249
   how to use, 224–25
Triceps, 158–65
   dip on chair, 162, *163*
   gym option: cable triceps pull-down, 161, *162*
   one-arm French press, 160, *161*
   one-arm press, 158, *159*
   one-arm press, warm up, 87
   sequencing exercise, 52

Upper body workout. See Arm exercises; Back exercises; Biceps; Chest exercises; Shoulder exercises; Training log

Warming up, 85–98
Water intake recommended, 260–61
Weight gain, aerobics and, 1–2
Weight loss
   aerobics ineffective, 1
   strength training, amount of reduction, 3–4
Weights
   amount of, and number of reps, 43, 225
   free, types of, 59, *59*
   increasing and periodization, 55–56
   machines, 60, *60*
   machines vs. free weight debate, 67–69
   soup cans, ix
"Working to failure," 41, 225

Yoga, 85

You've read about it — now let Kathy show you how lifting weights gives you a stronger, leaner body!

Try these or any other of Kathy's workouts on VHS and DVD, available wherever videos are sold!

"Lifting weights adds lean muscle to boost your metabolism and helps burn more calories all day long! In addition to toning and sculpting for a great-looking body, using weights increases bone density helping to improve posture and prevent osteoporosis. With my TimeSaver approach, you can get all these benefits in a quick workout that's fun and easy to do!"

- Kathy Smith

 Visit Kathy online at www.kathysmith.com and www.sonymusicvideo.com

© 2003 Sony Music Entertainment Inc./ ℗ Sony Music Entertainment and the KATHY SMITH logo are trademarks.

About the Author

KATHY SMITH has been a visionary in the fitness industry for more than twenty years. She is among the top sellers of fitness videos, audiotapes, books, and equipment and writes a nationally syndicated news column and a column for *Self* magazine, supporting her mission of educating consumers on being healthy and fit. Smith's twenty-six award-winning videos have sold more than eleven million copies around the world, earning her a place in the Video Hall of Fame. She has been at the forefront of promoting sports and fitness to America's youth and serves on the board of directors of the highly acclaimed University Elementary School at the University of California, Los Angeles. She is also a national ambassador for the March of Dimes. Smith is currently a member of the Woman's Sports Foundation's board of stewards, and she served on the board of trustees from 1993 to 1996. Her company, Kathy Smith Lifestyles, established a scholarship fund through the Woman's Sports Foundation in the name of her two daughters, Kate and Perrie, which demonstrates Smith's ongoing commitment to promoting sports and fitness to young girls. *Kathy Smith's Lift Weights to Lose Weight* is Smith's fourth book. Her previous three were *Kathy Smith's Getting Better All the Time*, *Kathy Smith's Fitness Makeover*, and *Kathy Smith's WalkFit for a Better Body*.

Made in the USA
Middletown, DE
16 December 2019